Hamlyn all-colour paperbacks

Electronics

Roland Worcester

Illustrated by
Design Practitioners

Hamlyn Paperbacks

FOREWORD

The science of electronics has revolutionized science and industry. It is bringing ever wider and faster changes. Computers can digest masses of statistics almost on the instant, or perform mathematical calculations with breathtaking speed. Electronic devices can soar with space vehicles through unimaginable distances, can probe and examine and send back pictures and reports from outer space. Everywhere electronics is at work – for example, in medicine, building, accountancy, metallurgy, telecommunications, manufacturing, industry – calculating, checking, testing, stopping, starting, watching, and carrying out many other functions.

Here is an introductory guide that gives the essentials of how it's done. The author follows the sound practice of illustrating principles by describing actual circuits, with careful explanations of what each component does. The opening chapters are devoted to statements of first principles. Then follow sections on radio, TV, tapes, radar, electronic controls, and various techniques.

Undoubtedly the development of electronic science is one of the major modern phenomena – and there is more, far more, to come. Hence the general reader owes it to himself to find out what electronics is all about, and this is one need that the book has been written to supply. Other readers must go far more deeply into the subject, or will find that electronics is a fascinating world which they are eager to explore further, and for these the book should provide an excellent starting-point.

Published by The Hamlyn Publishing Group Limited
London · New York · Sydney · Toronto
Astronaut House, Feltham, Middlesex, England

Copyright © The Hamlyn Publishing Group Limited 1969
Revised edition 1971
Tenth printing 1981

ISBN 0 600 00113 X
Phototypeset by BAS Printers Limited, Wallop, Hampshire
Colour separations by Schwitter Limited, Zurich
Printed in Spain by Mateu Cromo, Madrid

CONTENTS

INTRODUCTION: OUR ELECTRONIC WORLD

Electronics is the tool of today. It has given us radar, automation, space vehicles, radio telescopes, and a host of other inventions that have transformed our lives.

Electronics means putting electrons to work. An electron is one of the particles in an atom, and travels at incredible speed round the nucleus. Also of the first importance are the facts that the electron has a negative charge, the nucleus a positive one.

Many devices are explained in this book. For example, transformers couple circuits, transform or change one voltage to another, or perform other useful functions. Resistors and other circuit elements are described with electronic circuit diagrams which readily show the essential information about a piece of equipment. Again, a transistor is a device made from semiconductor material, e.g. a tiny slice of germanium or silicon. It allows a small current (between base and emitter) to control a large current (between emitter and collector). It is used in TV, in computers, and in many other devices.

4

In cathode ray tubes, an electron beam is deflected by electric or magnetic fields, and passes over the face of the tube. These tubes are employed in TV receivers, oscilloscopes and other equipment.

Electronic devices can send us information from satellites and space vehicles. Radio telescopes scan the heavens, gathering information from distances far beyond the range of visual observation.

Radar bounces radio signals off distant objects, and uses the echo to give information on their distance and direction. Sonar in ships uses sound-wave echoes for depth sounding.

Solar cells produce current when they are illuminated, giving power for space instruments. Light-sensitive diodes and transistors respond to light-pulses, and control electrical circuits by light. Other diodes produce light under the influence of an electric current. In fact, the skill of the electronics engineer makes of electrons in motion an almost magical tool.

And there are still many exciting challenges to be met as he carries on his research and devises fresh applications.

SOME BASIC FACTS

Electrons in Motion

We can make a picture of an atom as simple or as complicated as we like. We can show a hydrogen atom as a central nucleus or proton, circled by a single electron [1]. The proton has a positive charge, and is 1,840 times the mass of the electron, which has a negative charge.

The electron circles the nucleus millions of times in a millionth of a second, and hundreds of millions of atoms side by side would be needed to occupy an inch of space. Positive and negative charges (proton and electron) neutralize each other, so the atom has no surplus charge.

Helium has two electrons and two protons. The heavier elements have more and more electrons [2]. Uranium has 92. But normally there is no surplus charge, because the negative electrons are balanced by the positive charge of the nucleus.

There are other particles besides protons and electrons. The neutron has no charge and is found in some atoms. Other transitory particles arise, change their state, or apparently disappear in energy.

A hydrogen atom electron can absorb a photon or light particle, and take energy from it, moving to an orbit at a higher energy level. Or electrons may collapse to lower energy levels, emitting photons.

Surplus Charge

We have seen that, normally, the negative electron charge equals the positive nucleus charge: hence the atom has no surplus charge. However, sometimes an atom may gain an electron, and then it has a surplus negative charge. If an atom loses an electron, the nucleus protons are more numerous than the negative electrons, so the atom has a surplus positive charge. With semiconductors, we may speak of positive 'holes' or hole carriers. These can be imagined as spaces which could be occupied by negative electrons.

A body with a considerable excess of electrons has a strong negative charge; one with few electrons has a strong positive charge [3]. Thus there is a difference of potential, which exists so long as there is no means of electrons escaping, or nuclei gaining the electrons they lack.

If something allowing a free movement of electrons is placed between the negative and the positive charges, electrons move along this conductive path to occupy the nuclei which lack electrons [4]. This movement is an electric current, and it can take place through any conductor, such as a wire.

The Electric Current

If the movement of electrons is to be maintained, we must generate or produce a continuous surplus, which replaces electrons travelling away along the conductor. In equipment current can flow from battery negative to a lamp or other apparatus, then back along a second conductor to battery positive. The conducting leads, etc. form a 'circuit'.

The surplus of electrons at one terminal of the circuit can be produced and can be maintained chemically

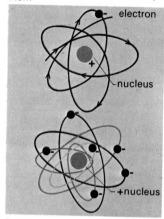

1 Simple picture of a hydrogen atom

electron

nucleus

+nucleus

2 Heavier atoms have more electrons

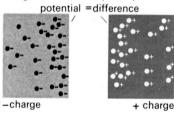

3 Potential differences between charges of dissimilar polarity

potential = difference

−charge   + charge

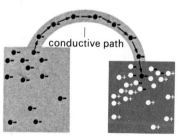

conductive path

4 Negative electrons flowing to influence the positive charge

by a battery. This is very handy for portable equipment. Or it may be produced electromagnetically by a generator. Again, photoelectric cells produce current under the stimulus of photons, or light particles, whilst a thermocouple, or junction of different metals, produces current when its temperature is raised.

Conductors

We use conductors to take current to the point where it is wanted. A conductor readily allows the free exchange of orbital electrons, so electrons forming the electric current can move from atom to atom along the material [5]. Silver and copper are good conductors, for they allow current to flow freely. Copper is drawn into wires, which may be wound into coils or used to carry current [6].

Insulators

We may need to direct current along a chosen path, and prevent it going elsewhere. Insulators help to do this. An

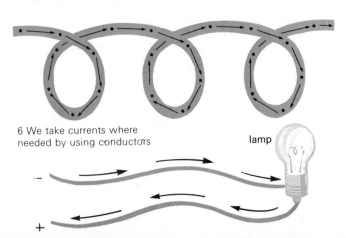

conducting material

5 Easy exchange of electrons forms current

6 We take currents where needed by using conductors

lamp

−

+

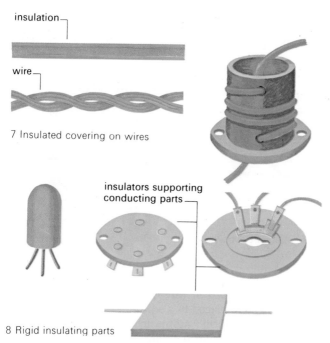

insulation

wire

7 Insulated covering on wires

insulators supporting
conducting parts

8 Rigid insulating parts

insulator is a material which does not readily allow the passage of an electric current. A perfect insulator would allow no exchange of electrons. Hence there would be no movement from atom to atom, and no current would flow. Glass, mica and rubber are good insulators, but so are many other substances. Rubber, polyvinyl chloride, cotton, silk, enamel or other insulating material on wires prevents the wires touching each other or nearby metal parts where current is not wanted [7].

Glass, mica, ceramic, phenolic plastic and other rigid insulating parts support conducting items in switches, valveholders, transistors, capacitors and many other electronic components [8].

What is the best kind of insulator depends on the work it must do. Insulators on wires may need to be thin and flexible. Insulating parts may have to be very strong, or may have to withstand high voltages, or high temperatures.

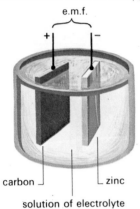

9 Simple cell generates electromotive force chemically

e.m.f.

+ −

carbon ⌐ ⌐ zinc

solution of electrolyte

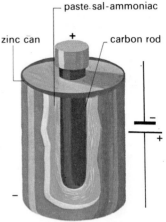

10 Popular dry cell

paste sal-ammoniac

zinc can

+ carbon rod

Primary Cells

We said that a potential difference can be produced chemically. Primary cells or batteries do this. If zinc and carbon plates are placed in a solution of sal-ammoniac [9] this happens. Chlorine atoms in the sal-ammoniac take incomplete atoms from the zinc, but each atom removed leaves two electrons. So a surplus of electrons, or negative charge, arises on the zinc.

The removed zinc atoms enter the solution as positive ions, or atoms lacking some electrons, until the solution can accept no more. The solution then has a positive charge and so has the carbon plate immersed in contact with it.

A potential difference or electromotive force (e.m.f.) now exists between the zinc and carbon plates. If a wire is connected from zinc to carbon, electrons flow through it. Chemical action maintains surplus electrons at the zinc until the cell is discharged.

The popular 'dry' Leclanché cell has a zinc canister as negative electrode and central carbon rod as the positive [10]. The rod is surrounded by powdered carbon and manganese dioxide, whose molecules can combine with hydrogen molecules to produce water and prevent hydrogen accumulating. The e.m.f. is about 1·5 volts.

10

Batteries

If the cell is large, there is more area for chemical action, and a more powerful current is available. If cells have the carbon rods and also the zinc cases joined [11], this is electrically like a larger cell. Voltage is that of a single cell.

If cells are joined positive to negative, the cells are in series [12]. The battery voltage is that of the cells added together – 3 volts for two 1·5 volt cells, and so on. A layer battery [12] has flat units placed one upon another. Miniature mercury cells are made for small apparatus.

Secondary cells or accumulators are re-charged by passing direct current through them from a generator or other supply. A vehicle accumulator usually has spongy lead and lead peroxide plates in dilute sulphuric acid, and each cell has an e.m.f. of 2 volts. Six cells form a 12 volt battery.

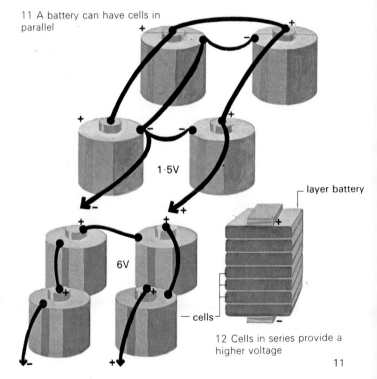

11 A battery can have cells in parallel

1·5V

layer battery

6V

cells

12 Cells in series provide a higher voltage

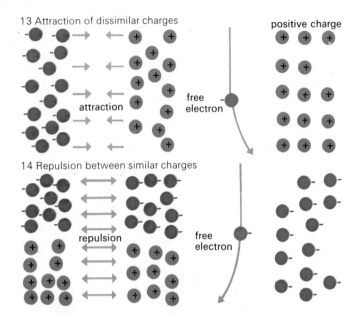

13 Attraction of dissimilar charges

positive charge

attraction

free electron

14 Repulsion between similar charges

repulsion

free electron

Free Electrons

Negative electrons try to move towards a positive charge [13]. If a free electron is moving near a positive charge, its path is curved, because of this attraction.

Repulsion exists between charges of the same polarity [14]. The path of a free electron or stream of electrons curves away from a negative charge. These effects are used to direct the electron stream in various electronic devices, such as the cathode ray tube used in oscilloscopes.

The path of a free electron is also changed by a magnetic field. TV tubes and magnetrons utilize this.

Electron Gun

A stream of electrons is obtained from an electron gun having a cathode heated by an internal filament [15]. The high temperature causes thermionic emission of electrons. The beam passes through a hole in a cylinder, its intensity controlled by potential applied. Making the cylinder negative repels electrons, reduces the beam.

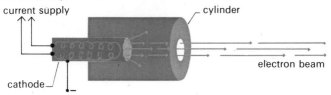

15 Electron gun emits stream of electrons

current supply

cylinder

cathode

electron beam

Focusing

A convex optical lens will focus light rays to a point. An electron lens has a similar effect on the cathode ray beam, the electric field curvature acting in much the same way as the glass lens on light rays [16]. Cylinders having different potentials have a similar effect.

By controlling the potential on one or more electrodes, the intensity of the field and its curvature can be adjusted, to focus the stream of electrons into a narrow beam.

The cathode ray tube has an electron gun, grid or aperture to control beam intensity, and accelerator and focusing electrodes. The beam strikes a fluorescent coating, producing a spot of light visible on the tube.

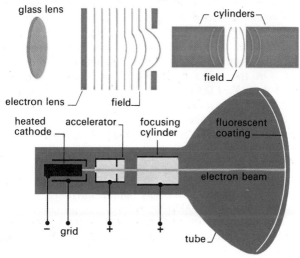

16 Focusing the beam in a cathode ray tube

glass lens

cylinders

field

electron lens

field

heated cathode

accelerator

focusing cylinder

fluorescent coating

electron beam

grid

tube

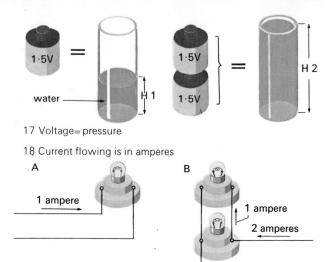

17 Voltage= pressure

18 Current flowing is in amperes

A

1 ampere

B

1 ampere

2 amperes

Circuit Laws and Units

A volt (V) is the unit of *pressure* from a battery or from some other source. A dry cell has a pressure of 1·5 volts. Two cells in series provide 1·5+1·5=3 volts. A vessel half full has a depth of water H1 [17]. The depth H2 is twice H1. A pipe from the bottom of the second vessel delivers water at twice the pressure of the first vessel. Similarly, raising the voltage increases electrical pressure.

Some circuits operate at low voltage. Others require hundreds or thousands of volts. 1,000 volts=1 kilovolt, or 1kV. On the other hand, very low voltages are in millivolts or mV. 1,000mV=1V. Extremely low voltages are in microvolts, or μV. 1,000μV=1mV.

The ampere (A) is the magnitude of current flow. For example, a bulb could take 1A [18a]. Two such bulbs take 1 ampere each, or 2 amperes, or twice as much current [18b].

Small currents are given in milliamperes, or mA. 1,000mA=1 ampere. Extremely small currents are in microamperes, or μA. 1,000μA=1mA.

The ohm (Ω) is the unit of *resistance*. A thick wire has little resistance and lets current pass readily [19]. In the same way a large pipe lets water flow easily. A thin wire resists the ready flow of current, just as the small pipe offers resistance to the flow of water. The greater the electrical resistance of a component or circuit, the more the passage of current is hindered.

Copper wires have little resistance, so they let current pass readily. But we may want resistance in many circuits. Iron and alloy wires can provide this. Making the wire thinner or increasing its length raises the resistance. Carbon compounds resist the ready flow of current, and can be formed into rods having any resistance needed. They are widely used. A component having resistance is a 'resistor' [20]. A variable resistor has a sliding contact, bringing into circuit as much of the resistance element as is wanted. A potentiometer has a connection at each end and sliding contact.

For high values we use $k\Omega$, or kilo-ohm. $1k = 1,000$ ohms. Very high values are in $M\Omega$ (megohms). $1\ M\Omega = 1,000k$. Resistors are usually colour-coded. Each colour shows a figure, or a number of noughts.

19 Ohm = unit of resistance

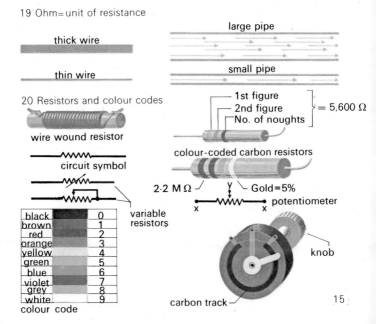

thick wire

large pipe

thin wire

small pipe

20 Resistors and colour codes

wire wound resistor

1st figure
2nd figure
No. of noughts
} = 5,600 Ω

circuit symbol

colour-coded carbon resistors

2·2 MΩ   Gold = 5%

potentiometer

variable resistors

colour	code
black	0
brown	1
red	2
orange	3
yellow	4
green	5
blue	6
violet	7
grey	8
white	9

colour code

knob

carbon track

15

Ohm's Law

If we increase the voltage applied to a circuit, the current flowing becomes stronger [21]. Reducing the voltage makes the current weaker.

If we leave the voltage the same, increasing the resistance will make the current weaker [22]. Reducing the resistance naturally allows more current to flow.

These facts are the basis of Ohm's Law. We say:

Current in Amperes × Resistance in Ohms = Volts
As I is used for current, and R for ohms, this is $I \times R = V$,
or $IR = V$. In the same way, $\frac{V}{I} = R$ and $\frac{V}{R} = I$

Always remember that the basic units are amperes, volts and ohms. As an example, 1mA flows through 100k. What voltage is dropped? 1mA = 0·001 ampere, and 100k = 100,000 ohms. So 0·001 × 100,000 = 100 volts.

The *power* that is usefully employed or perhaps wasted or dissipated in a circuit is given in watts. Useful power could raise the temperature of valve heaters, or operate a loudspeaker or other device. Wasted power might be that lost in a resistor which is fitted to reduce the voltage.

21 Current increases with voltage

22 Increasing resistance reduces current

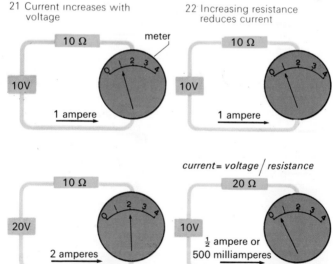

current = voltage / resistance

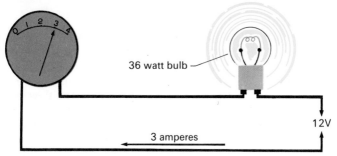

23 Electrical power in a circuit (Power=watts=voltage × current)

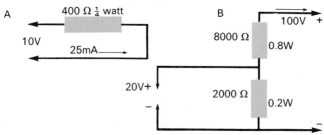

24 Voltage; resistance, current and wattage

We could give the useful output of an amplifier or other device in watts. Small powers are given in milliwatts. 1,000mW = 1 watt. Power in watts = voltage × current.

Voltage in Volts × Current in Amperes = Watts

Or we can say $\frac{Watts}{Volts}$ = *Amperes* or $\frac{Watts}{Amperes}$ = *Volts*

A 36 watt car bulb is run from a 12 volt battery [23]. So

it draws $\frac{36}{12}$ = 3 amperes current.

Imagine that a potential of 10 volts is present across a 400 ohm resistor [24a].

From $I = \frac{Volts}{Resistance} = \frac{10}{400} = 0 \cdot 025$ ampere.

With resistors in series, 8,000 ohms + 2,000 ohms = 10,000 ohms [24b] From $I = \frac{V}{R}$ or $\frac{100}{10,000}$ we find that 10mA (0·01A) flows.

The Inductor

An inductor is a coil of wire. When current begins to flow, a magnetic field arises which tries to hinder the flow of current. When the current ceases or changes direction, the magnetic field collapses, and produces an electromotive force (e.m.f.) which tries to maintain the flow of current. The inductor is trying to prevent *changes* in current. In Figure 25a inductor A is connected to an alternating current supply – that is, one which changes direction rapidly. The inductor shown in [25b] has more turns and opposes the flow of current more strongly. The inductor with more turns has more 'inductance'. The extent to which it impedes the flow of current is its 'reactance' (in ohms).

In Figure 26a the supply has a frequency of 50 cycles per second, or 50 c/s (also called 50 Hertz, or 50Hz). It goes through its cycle of changing direction one way then the other 50 times in each second. At [26b] the frequency is 100 hertz. The reactance of the same inductor is twice that at A. Reactance increases as frequency increases.

The 'henry' is the unit of inductance. Smaller values are given in mH (millihenrys) and μH (microhenrys).

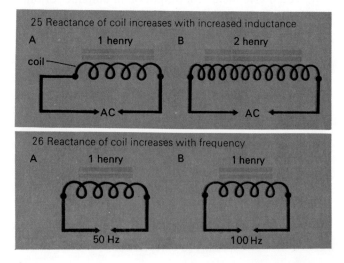

25 Reactance of coil increases with increased inductance

A   1 henry   B   2 henry

coil

→AC←

→ AC ←

26 Reactance of coil increases with frequency

A   1 henry   B   1 henry

50 Hz   100 Hz

Reactance of Capacitor

A capacitor has plates insulated from each other. If we connect an e.m.f., a charge surges into the capacitor. If we remove the e.m.f. and connect a wire across the capacitor, the stored charge surges out. (See page 28).

If we connect an alternating source to the capacitor, current surges in and out each time the polarity changes. The capacitor hinders the flow of current. This is called the 'reactance' and is in ohms.

In Figure 27a, AC is connected to the capacitor and a certain current flows. If we make the capacitor larger [27b], the current is larger too, because the reactance is lower. Reactance falls with an increase in capacitance. In Figure 28a we apply 50 hertz AC to the capacitor. At [28b], we apply 100 Hz. The reactance of the same capacitor is lower with B. Reactance falls with increased frequency.

Does it Matter?

Figure 29 shows a transformer (see page 40). Primary P takes audio signals from amplifier; secondary S supplies loudspeaker. Capacitor C is across the primary. Higher

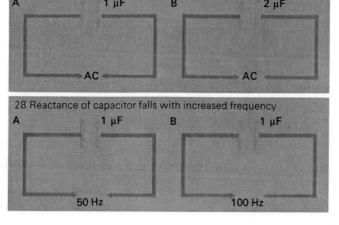

27 Reactance of capacitor falls with increased capacity

A   1 µF   B   2 µF

AC   AC

28 Reactance of capacitor falls with increased frequency

A   1 µF   B   1 µF

50 Hz   100 Hz

frequencies more readily pass through C and do not flow through the primary. This acts as a 'top cut' tone control.

In Figure 30 capacitor C1 is from an audio amplifier valve anode, and by-passes or loses higher frequencies to earth.

The effect is changed by placing part of the variable resistor VR1 in circuit. VR1 is a variable top cut tone control.

29 Falling reactance of capacitor 'cuts' high frequencies

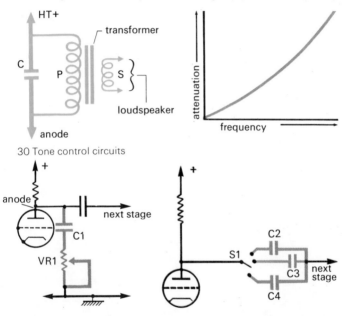

30 Tone control circuits

The switch S1 selects a small capacitor C2, a medium value capacitor C3, or a large capacitor C4, C2 lets high frequencies pass easily. C3 lets more lower frequencies pass. C4 allows low frequencies to pass readily. Tone controls are often found in receivers and amplifiers. Most make use of the fact that capacitive reactance falls with increased frequency.

Inductive reactance also has many uses. In Figure 31 a rectifier supplies a power filter. Output from the rectifier

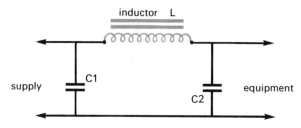

has pronounced ripple. L is a choke with high inductance. It hinders fluctuations in current. Capacitor C1 acts as a reservoir. The inductor L refuses to let ripples pass, and capacitor C2 provides almost pure direct current. This is called 'smoothing'.

In Figure 32a radio frequency (RF) signals and audio frequency (AF) signals arise at collector C. The radio frequency choke hinders RF, so this goes through the small capacitor C1. The choke reactance is low at low frequency, so AF passes through it and is taken off by the larger capacitor C2.

At [32b], a high frequency hiss filter choke is placed in an audio circuit. It does not let high frequencies pass, and so reduces surface hiss when playing records.

32 Blocking the movement of high frequencies

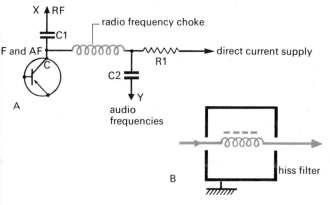

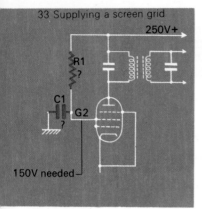

33 Supplying a screen grid

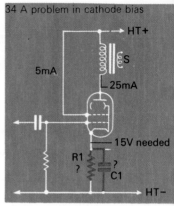

34 A problem in cathode bias

A pentode valve as amplifier is shown in Figure 33. The supply line is 250 volts, but the valve screen grid G2 should have only 150 volts. Since $250-150=100$, resistor R1 should drop 100 volts.

The current flowing through R1 is measured or found from the valve-maker's information. It is 5mA. Recalling that $\frac{V}{I}=R$, we can say that $\frac{100}{0.005}=20,000$ ohms for R1.

What power is dissipated in R1?

$Watts=V\times I=100\times0.005=0.5$ watt. So we fit a 20k $\frac{1}{2}$-watt resistor. G2 needs to be 'earthed' at working frequency. So C1 is a 0.05 μF 250 volt capacitor.

At the output stage of the receiver, 15 volts should be present at the cathode [34]. Cathode current is $25+5$mA $=$ 30mA or 0.03A.

$$\text{So R1 is } \frac{15}{0.03}=500 \text{ ohms.}$$

For audio frequencies and 15 volts, C1 can be 25 μF 25 volts working.

A test instrument for two voltage ranges – 0 to 10 volts and 0 to 100 volts – is shown in Figure 35. For a full-scale reading, 1mA must flow (0.001A). This is to show 10 volts with R1. R1 $=\frac{10}{0.001}=10,000$ ohms. Similarly, R2 $=$ 100,000 ohms.

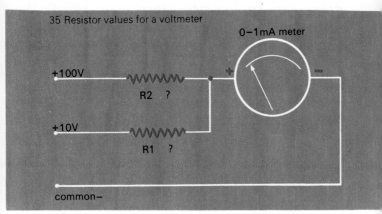

35 Resistor values for a voltmeter

0-1mA meter

+100V R2 ?

+10V R1 ?

common−

36 DC working conditions of a transistor amplifier

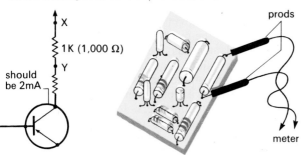

X

1K (1,000 Ω)

Y

should be 2mA

prods

meter

A transistor circuit where we suspect the transistor is not drawing a correct collector current, though all resistors and the supply voltage are correct, is shown in Figure 36. The collector current should be 2mA. The simplest test is to measure the voltage across the resistor, from X to Y. From $V = I \times R$, the voltage should be $0 \cdot 002 \times 1,000 = 2$ volts.

A meter reads only $0 \cdot 5$ volt.

$$\text{From } I = \frac{V}{R} = \frac{0 \cdot 5}{1,000}$$

we see that the transistor collector current is actually $0 \cdot 5$mA.

23

Electronic Circuit Diagrams

For some electronic equipment, components could be shown in outline, with connections, in a scale drawing just as in the apparatus.

But it is usually better to have a circuit diagram where simple symbols represent various components. Symbols are often simplified representations of the components. By comparing components and their symbols, you will become familiar with them.

Lines represent wires. These may be joined as in Figure 37a. They may cross without contact [37b]. Dots [37c] show connecting points such as sockets, which could be for plugs connected to a loudspeaker, or could be used for some other purpose.

A fixed resistor symbol is shown in Figure 38, together with three resistors in a small part of a circuit. In Figures 39a and 39b is shown a variable resistor. If connections are taken to X and Y, moving the sliding contact (arrow) to the right increases the resistance actually in circuit.

The resistance element may be wire for low values, but is carbon for high values. The track can be in a semi-circle, and rotating a spindle moves the contact along the track [39c]. Figure 39d is a typical component.

B, C and D are potentiometers. If a potential – such as an audio signal voltage – is taken to X and Z, any required level can be tapped off by moving slider Y. This happens with an audio volume control.

Switches

In Figure 40 is shown an on/off switch. It could be a mains voltage toggle switch, low voltage rotary switch, or any other component.

A volume control often has a switch. It can be a single on/off type (single pole), or it can be two on/off switches (double pole) which work together to interrupt two circuits.

The rotary switch in Figure 40 has a contact X, which can transfer a circuit to 1, 2 or 3, the switch having three positions. It is '1-pole 3-way'. It could have more contacts and more ways, as required.

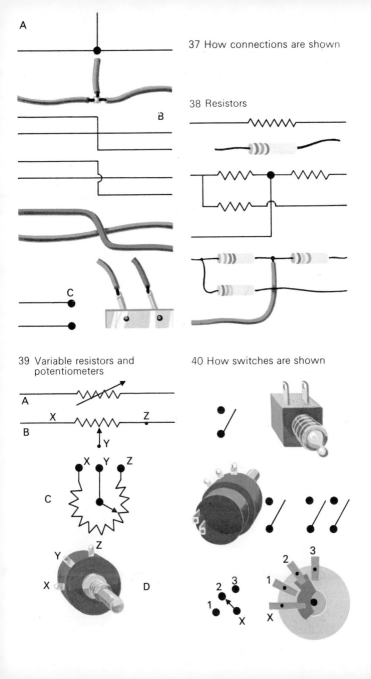

A 37 How connections are shown

38 Resistors

B

C

39 Variable resistors and potentiometers

A

B X Z

Y

C X Y Z

D Y Z X

40 How switches are shown

2 3
1 X

2 3
1 X

Inductors and Coils

Insulated wire wound upon an insulated tube forms a coil or inductor [41]. We can increase the inductance by using more turns, or having a larger coil. Or we can place a core in the winding to concentrate the magnetic field and raise its inductance.

The inductor might be of very small inductance and have few turns [42a]. Larger inductance coils have more turns [42b]. The coil could have a tapped winding – or two or more windings on the same insulated tube [42c]. If there are very many turns they may be in sections [42d]. This is a 'high frequency choke' – an inductor which prevents the passage of high frequencies.

Special materials have to be used for cores for radio frequency coils (those that work at radio frequencies). A core of ferrite or iron dust material placed in the coil winding intensifies the magnetic field and raises the inductance, so if we want to adjust the inductance, we can

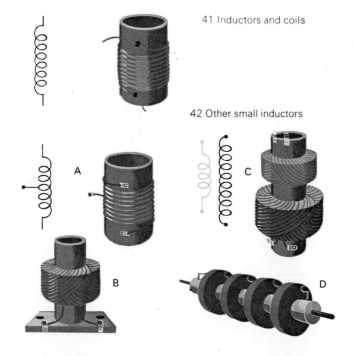

41 Inductors and coils

42 Other small inductors

use a threaded core, and screw it in or out [43]. In the symbol, the dotted line is the core, and the sloping line shows it is adjustable. To simplify large circuit diagrams, cores are often not shown.

LF Cores

At low frequencies, cores can be made from various alloys [44]. Thin sheet iron was once used.

The winding is often on a bobbin, entirely surrounded by the core. One limb fits inside the winding. This core is often of thin metal 'stampings' or laminations, and enough are used to make up the thickness wanted.

Since this inductor prevents the ready flow of low frequencies it is a 'low frequency choke'. Such a choke is often employed to help remove ripple in a supply from a power circuit, and is then called a 'smoothing choke'. In order to be used for this purpose, it would normally have an inductance of several henrys.

43 Adjustable core allows inductance to be changed

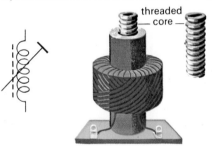

44 Large inductor with core made from laminations

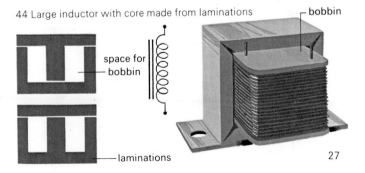

Capacitors

Two metal plates near each other but not in contact form a capacitor and can store a charge [45]. If we connect a voltage to X-X a deficiency of electrons arises at one plate, and a surplus at the other. Electrostatic stress arises in the insulating space between plates. The capacitor is 'charged' with a power depending on 'capacity' or charge-storing ability. Unit of capacitance = farad (F).

If X-X are joined together, the capacitor gives up its charge. We can increase the capacity to hold a charge by placing the plates nearer each other, and in other ways. The insulation between plates is the 'dielectric'. Capacitors are made with mica and ceramic insulation, or foil rolled up with insulating paper and in a tube [46]. Or metallic conductors may be deposited on an insulator.

'Electrolytic' capacitors are so made that an applied voltage must be of the correct polarity. These capacitors are of some set value and are called 'fixed capacitors'.

We may need to change the capacitance at any time and

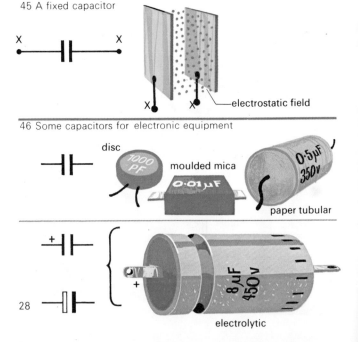

45 A fixed capacitor

X   X

X   X   electrostatic field

46 Some capacitors for electronic equipment

disc

1000 PF

moulded mica

0·01 μF

0·5 μF 350 v

paper tubular

+

8 μF 450 v

28

electrolytic

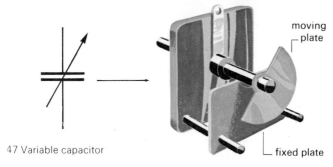

47 Variable capacitor

moving plate
fixed plate

48 2-gang and trimmer capacitors

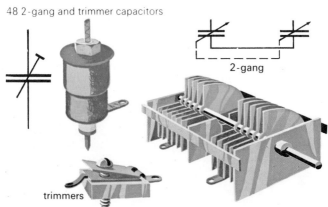

2-gang

trimmers

for this we want a 'variable capacitor'. A small variable capacitor can have one fixed plate, and one moving plate attached to a spindle [47]. Rotating the spindle changes the extent to which moving and fixed plates overlap each other, and thus alters the capacity. Capacity is least with the plates not overlapping at all.

We may wish to tune two circuits simultaneously in a radio receiver and can then use a 2-gang capacitor [48]. By having many fixed and many moving plates, the total capacity of each section can be increased. Sometimes the capacity has to be adjusted when first putting a circuit into proper working condition. A 'trimmer' is then used. It is adjusted with a screwdriver or other tool, and brings moving and fixed plates closer to increase the capacity.

An Amplifier

The circuit in Figure 49 is the first audio amplifier stage of a receiver or large audio amplifier. It increases the voltage of audio signals obtained from a pick-up employed to play records, or from a receiver detector.

Capacitor C1 isolates earlier direct current circuits from the base B of the transistor, supplied by the resistors R1 and R2. Resistor R3 applies a small negative bias to the emitter E. Bias increases when emitter current rises. This helps to make working conditions stable. C2 grounds the emitter E at audio frequencies.

Current from collector C flows through resistor R4. Amplified signal voltages are developed across R4. Signals are taken off by capacitor C3.

A practical layout of Figure 49 is shown in Figure 50a. Figure 50b is the same amplifier assembled in more compact form.

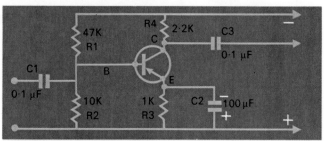

49 One-stage transistor amplifier

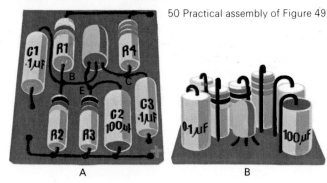

50 Practical assembly of Figure 49

Block Diagrams

We may show the essential parts of a circuit without going into detail. Block diagrams do this. Figure 51 is a block diagram of a large amplifier. Each 'box' represents one section – Section 1 is an audio frequency amplifier like Figure 49. So is Section 2. Section 3 is an output stage, or amplifier which supplies appreciable power. Signals reach it from Section 2, and its output goes to the loudspeaker.

Figure 52a is for playing stereo records. The stereo pick-up produces left-hand and right-hand channel signals. These go to the balancing section, where the relative volume is adjusted. Amplifiers supply outputs for right-hand and left-hand speakers.

Figure 52b is a block diagram showing a photoelectric merchandise counter. Merchandise interrupts light falling on the cell, causing electrical output to work a counter.

51 Block diagram of audio amplifier

52 Block diagrams of stereo amplifier and photo-electric counter

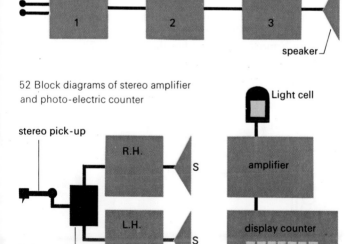

A   B   31

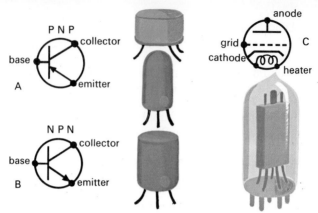

53 Transistor symbols and thermionic triode

Other Symbols

The symbol for a PNP transistor is shown in Figure 53a; that for the NPN transistor at 53b. Figure 53c is the symbol for a triode valve. The valve might be of any type.

Remember, most symbols are simplified representations of the component or its function! The relay [54] illustrates this. Tags X-X take current to an electromagnet winding. The spring-actuated contact Y normally rests against the fixed contact 1. When current flows in the winding, the armature Y moves and switches the circuit to 2.

Sometimes items in a circuit can be omitted, to obtain a diagram which is easier to follow, or to ignore repeated details. In Figure 55 the switch allows inductor L1, L2, L3 or L4 to be selected. This is shown in full at [55a]. At [55b]

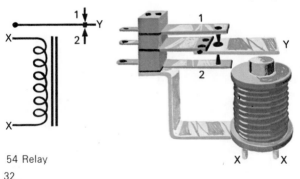

54 Relay

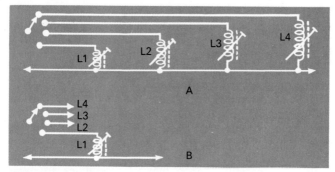

55 Omissions for clarity

the actual way in which inductor L1 is connected is shown and inductors L2, L3, and L4 are omitted.

Simplifications of this kind are very useful when there are several switch positions and sections, and possibly quite a large number of inductors or other parts.

Theoretical circuits do not usually take into account the actual way in which the equipment is assembled. For example, an amplifier circuit could be assembled on a panel and occupy quite a large space. Or it could be arranged on a smaller panel, with components close together, or made with miniature components to the smallest possible size. But in all these cases it might be the same circuit.

Various other symbols are shown in Figure 56.

56 Various other symbols

aerial battery light-dependent resistor cell

earth diode lamp

chassis or earth return Zener diode moving-coil speaker

Magnetism is Important

An unmagnetized bar has all its particles at random [57a]. Magnetizing it draws them into similar polarity [57b]. The bar magnet [57c] has a north pole at one end, and south pole at the other end. Other shapes are the horseshoe [57d] and ring magnets [57e].

If the north pole of one magnet is near the south pole of another magnet, an attractive force arises. But if a north pole is placed by a north pole, or a south pole by a south pole, a repulsive force tries to push the magnets apart. Both poles attract ferrous or iron objects.

Various specially shaped magnet assemblies are used [58]. That at Figure 58a has curved ends to accommodate the rotating coil of a meter; [58b] is for a similar purpose. Figure 58c is for a moving-coil speaker or microphone.

If we connect a coil to a battery or other direct current supply, a magnetic field is created [59a]. It has north and south poles, and exists so long as current flows. The

57 Permanent magnets

58 Shaped magnets for electronic apparatus

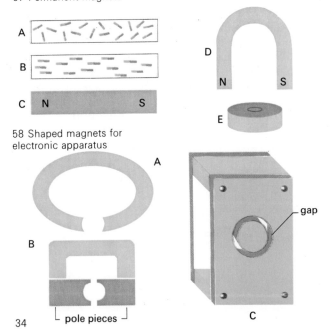

magnetic field arises when the switch is closed and current begins [59b]. When the switch is opened, the field collapses [59c]. This generates an electromotive force or e.m.f. in the coil, of opposite polarity to that from the battery. If the supply polarity is reversed, the magnetic poles are also reversed. If we connect the coil to an alternating current supply [60] current flows back and forth through the coil. At each reversal of direction, the magnetic field collapses and arises with opposite polarity. Most electromagnets have cores allowing concentration of magnetic force. Current in a winding creates a magnetic field.

The reverse arises. If a magnet is moved in or out of a coil, an e.m.f. is produced [61]. The magnetic field must be changing or in motion. The magnetic field can be from a permanent magnet, or from another electromagnet. These effects are used in generators, where the rapid motion of magnetic fields produces strong currents, as well as in other devices.

59 Field surrounding an inductor

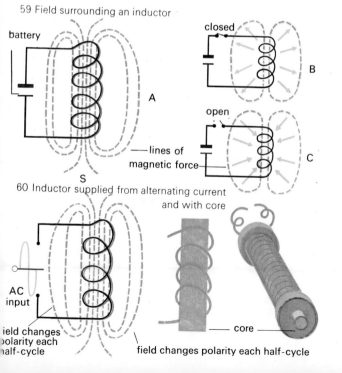

battery

closed

A

B

open

lines of
magnetic force

C

S

60 Inductor supplied from alternating current
and with core

AC
input

field changes
polarity each
half-cycle

core

field changes polarity each half-cycle

Moving-Coil Meter

In Figure 62, a strong field exists in the circular space between the shaped pole pieces. A coil is pivoted to rotate in this gap. Current is fed to it by hairsprings, and a pointer is attached.

When current flows in the coil, the magnetic field surrounding the conductors interacts with the permanent magnet field, and the coil rotates slightly. This can show current, voltage, or other things we wish to know. When current ceases, the coil returns to its original position.

61 Changing magnetic field generates e.m.f.

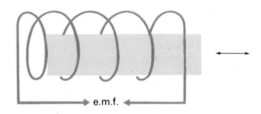

62 Moving-coil meter

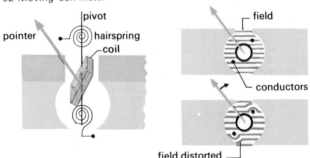

Moving-Coil Speaker

This embodies a cone carrying a very light coil, which receives current by flexible leads [63]. The coil occupies a narrow gap in a magnet assembly, and can move in and out in line with the cone axis.

Audio signals taken to the coil generate a fluctuating magnetic field. Interaction between this field and the fixed

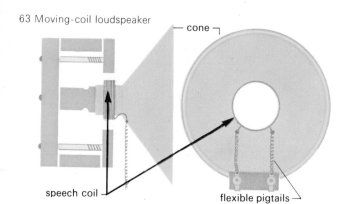

magnet field causes the coil and cone to move in and out. This is transmitted to the air, producing sound waves.

The winding is often called the 'speech coil'. 'Permanent magnet' moving-coil speakers have a permanent magnet assembly. 'Energized' speakers have an electromagnet, or winding, on the centre limb of the assembly, and current in this produces the magnetic field.

In a moving-coil microphone, vibrations of the cone and coil produce an e.m.f. in the coil.

'OR' Gate

Small cores are used for various purposes in computers. In Figure 64 an input at A OR at B will give an output. This is called an 'OR' gate.

64 Magnetic 'OR' gate for computer

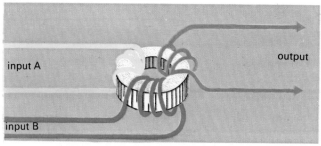

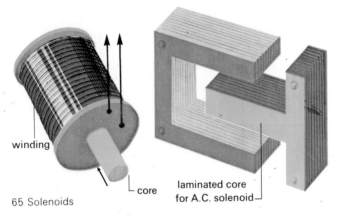

winding

core

laminated core
for A.C. solenoid

65 Solenoids

Solenoid and Magnetic Field

When current flows in a winding, a core becomes magnetized. If the core is out of the winding, magnetic forces endeavour to pull it in [65]. The limbs of the plunger and the fixed portion of the assembly can be shaped to assist this action by concentrating the magnetic field. A solenoid may control fuel or liquid flow valves, mechanical step-by-step counters, and many other devices.

Sometimes we wish to avoid magnetic fields, as in 'non-inductive' wire-wound resistors. Then we try to make one part of the field cancel another part [66]. Here, A is a wire-wound resistor, resembling an electromagnet. B has a loop: current reverses and flows back. C uses thin flat mica. One-half of each turn lies flat under the other half. D reverses the winding direction half-way.

Electrons are influenced by the presence of magnetic

66 Non-inductive wire-wound resistors

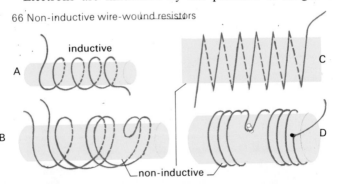

inductive

A

C

B

non-inductive

D

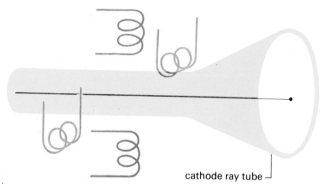

cathode ray tube

67 Magnetic deflection of cathode ray

fields. This is useful with television picture tubes, and with magnetrons, etc.

A stream of electrons is emitted by the electron gun of a cathode ray tube [67]. The beam passes between coils on the tube. When no current flows in these coils, the beam travels straight to the screen, and produces a central bright spot on the fluorescent coating.

Current flowing in the coils produces a field which curves the electron path up or down, or from side to side. In this way the beam is made to strike the screen at any point we want.

By altering the strength and polarity of current in the coils, the beam can be made to travel over any part of the picture-tube face. The coils are specially shaped to lie round the tube [68]. Electromagnetic deflection of the electron beam is widely used in TV receivers.

68 Arrangement of coils on cathode-ray tube

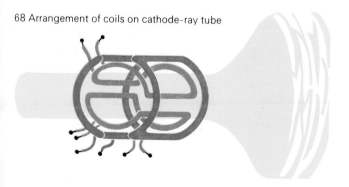

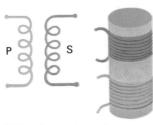

69 An air-cored transformer

70 Transformer with core

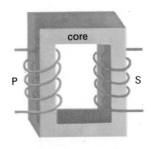

core

P   S

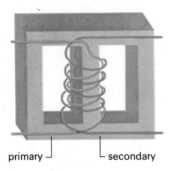

primary   secondary

Transformers

Transformers are useful devices relying on electromagnetic effects. They have two windings [69]. The primary (P) receives power from some source (an aerial, amplifier, or alternating current mains). The secondary (S) delivers power to a following device or circuit (a transistor or valve, a loudspeaker, a motor, an electric lamp, etc.)

The transformer may be 'air cored' for high frequencies [69] – that is, it may have no solid core material. Currents in the primary develop a fluctuating electromagnetic field, rising and falling rapidly according to the current. This field cuts the turns of the secondary, and induces an e.m.f. in the winding.

For lower frequencies, audio circuits, or alternating current mains, solid cores are placed in the windings. These concentrate the magnetic field, and are generally made up from thin laminations. (See also page 27.)

Primary and secondary may be on separate limbs of the core [70] or a bobbin fitted on the centre limb.

The transformer changes

or transforms one voltage to another, according to the 'turns ratio', or relationship between primary turns and secondary turns [71].

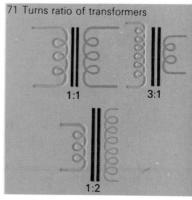

71 Turns ratio of transformers

If there were the same number of turns on primary and secondary and the transformer were perfectly efficient, the secondary would deliver the same voltage as applied to the primary. The ratio is 1:1. Or suppose the secondary has one-third the number of primary turns. The ratio is 3:1. If the primary received 240 volts AC, the secondary would deliver 80 volts. But if the secondary had twice as many turns as the primary, the ratio would be 1:2. If the primary received 240 volts, the secondary would give 480 volts.

Transformers produce the voltages we want, or couple circuits together. A transformer may have several windings [72]. The primary here is tapped for 210/230/250 volt mains. One secondary supplies 5 volts, another 6·3 volts, and a third 500 volts centre tapped, or 250/0/250 volts. That is, 250 volts each side of the tapping.

72 Typical mains transformer

250V
230V
210V

5V
250V
0V
250V

laminations forming core

6·3V

0

leads coloured for identification

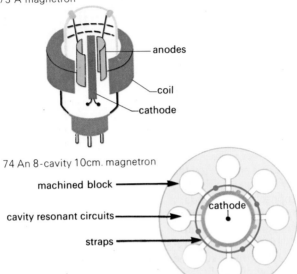

73 A magnetron

anodes

coil

cathode

74 An 8-cavity 10cm. magnetron

machined block

cavity resonant circuits

straps

cathode

output

The Magnetron

A small 2-anode magnetron – a device which can produce radio frequency energy – is shown in Figure 73. If no magnetic field were present, negative electrons would flow from cathode to positive anodes. When the magnetic field intensity is raised the electrons take curved paths and tend to circle the cathode.

An alternating potential is obtained on the anodes from a resonant circuit. Electrons approaching the higher potential anode accelerate. Those approaching the lower potential lose velocity, so that clusters of electrons tend to revolve round the cathode, maintaining the oscillation.

Operation is in brief duty periods (less than one per cent) with high power at high frequency. Large radar magnetrons deliver many thousands of watts, at centimetre wavelengths. For very high frequencies, the anodes are formed with cavities which act as the resonant circuit. Anodes and cavities are arranged in a ring [74].

Cyclotron

The cyclotron [75] can supply high-energy particles and has two D-shaped members. They are supplied with high frequency alternating current at many kilovolts. The whole is in a vacuum and placed between magnetic poles. Particles travel in a curved path because of the magnetic field. Particles approach each of the D-shaped members as the potential is rising, and this accelerates them. They travel round and round, gaining velocity until ejected through the opening. They bombard other particles, and facts are learned about the nucleus. The synchrotron, with magnets round a circular track, has accelerated particles up to nearly the speed of light. Particles generated include protons, deuterons and alpha particles.

Magnetohydrodynamics, or Gas Flow Electricity

If a conductor is moved across the lines of force of a magnetic field, an electromotive force is generated [76]. When a flow of ionized gas is directed between the poles of a magnet, an e.m.f. is also produced. Current can be taken away by conducting plates.

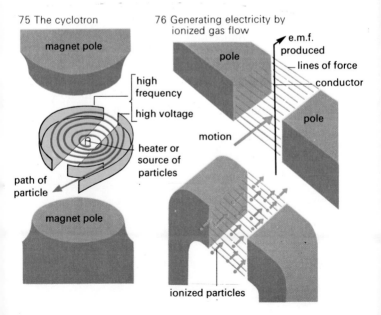

75 The cyclotron

magnet pole

high frequency

high voltage

heater or source of particles

path of particle

magnet pole

76 Generating electricity by ionized gas flow

e.m.f. produced

lines of force

conductor

pole

pole

motion

ionized particles

Heated Cathode Valves

A directly heated filament is a thin wire heated by an electric current. It then emits electrons.

Often we have the surface which emits electrons

77 Directly heated filament and indirectly heated cathode

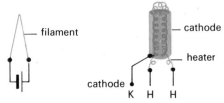

separated electrically from the filament [77]. The filament is electrically insulated from the tube or cathode, which reaches working temperature after an interval. The filament is the heater; the valves are 'indirectly heated'.

Diode

A thermionic diode has two essential electrodes, and it lets current pass one way only. The diode valve has a metal plate or anode by the cathode [78]. In working circuits we assume that current will be applied to the heater: so these connections are often omitted in diagrams.

If the anode has a positive voltage, electrons emitted by the cathode flow to the anode. If the anode is negative, electrons emitted by the cathode are not attracted. No current flows. The diode allows electrons to flow from cathode to anode, but not from anode to cathode.

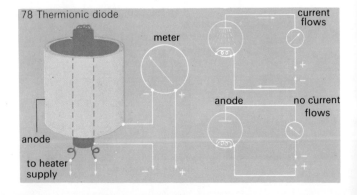

78 Thermionic diode

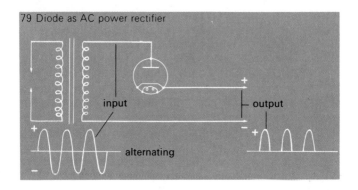

input

output

alternating

Diode Rectifier

Direct current flows steadily in one direction. Alternating current flows first one way, then the other. With 50 cycle per second mains there are 50 cycles each second [79]. If we apply this to a diode, current passes only during those intervals when the diode anode is positive. Half-cycles of opposite polarity are suppressed, so we obtain pulsating direct current.

A single diode has cathode and anode. This is also a 'half-wave rectifier'. A 'full-wave rectifier' [80] has two anodes, and can be connected to make use of both half-waves of the AC supply cycles.

80 A full-wave rectifier

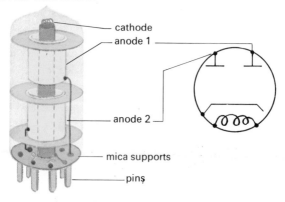

cathode

anode 1

anode 2

mica supports

pins

Diode Current

Suppose we provide any chosen voltage by moving the slider of a potentiometer VR [81]. A milliammeter indicates the diode current. As the voltage increases, more electrons are attracted to the anode, and current rises. When practically all the electrons are attracted, the current levels off, and scarcely increases at all, even with a much higher anode voltage. This is the maximum, or saturation current.

Full-Wave Rectification

A single diode in a half-wave rectification circuit allowed half-cycles of an alternating supply to flow, so we obtained pulsating direct current. Full-wave rectification is possible with two anodes or two separate single diodes [82]. The transformer secondary is centre-tapped. For one half-cycle one diode is positive, and for the other half-cycle the other diode is positive. So both half-cycles are utilized.

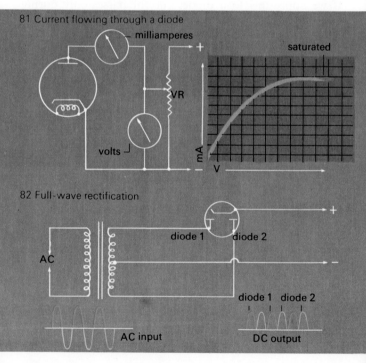

81 Current flowing through a diode

milliamperes

saturated

VR

volts

mA

V

82 Full-wave rectification

diode 1   diode 2

AC

diode 1   diode 2

AC input

DC output

Much AC mains equipment has a rectifier which supplies direct current for other valves. The pulsating DC has to be made steady and continuous. 'Smoothing capacitors' across the supply, and a 'smoothing choke' in series do this [83]. The capacitors store energy and give out current. The choke opposes changes in current. Thus a smooth supply, almost like that from a battery, is available.

Uses for Diodes

Thermionic diode power rectifiers [84] can supply large currents at high voltage. Smaller diodes provide detection or demodulation, or rectify signals for automatic volume control bias. With an indirectly heated cathode, heater and cathode can be connected to different circuits. But if it has a directly heated cathode or filament, there is no separate cathode connection. This can be important with power rectifiers.

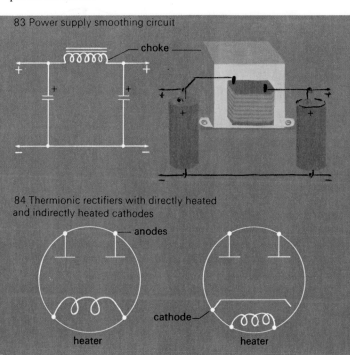

83 Power supply smoothing circuit

— choke —

84 Thermionic rectifiers with directly heated and indirectly heated cathodes

— anodes

cathode —

heater   heater

The Triode

A diode has two important electrodes: cathode and anode. The triode has a third electrode, a grid of thin wires, between cathode and anode [85]. Electrons flowing from cathode to anode pass between the meshes of the grid. The triode can 'amplify' signals, or increase their strength. If the grid is at or near zero potential it has little effect on the flow of electrons.

Suppose a meter placed between the anode and supply shows 8mA with −1 volt [86]. If we make the grid more negative, electrons are repelled from its vicinity, so that

85 A triode has control grid between cathode and anode

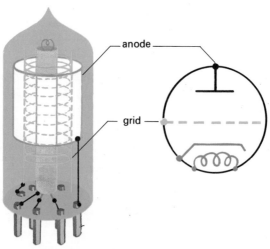

anode current is reduced. With −2 volts at the grid, anode current has fallen to about 6mA. At −3 volts current is 4mA. If the grid is made very negative, virtually all the electrons emitted by the cathode are repelled by the negative charge on it, and do not reach the anode.

Changes in grid voltage control the anode current, so it is called the 'control grid'. A steady voltage is called 'grid bias'. Changing the grid potential by 1 volt causes anode current to change by 2mA. The valve has a mutual conductance of 2mA per volt, or 2mA/V.

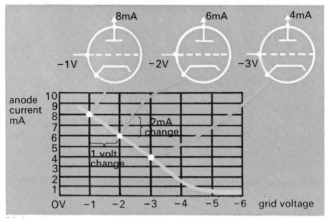

86 Anode current controlled by grid voltage

We can apply various anode voltages, and read anode current with a meter [87]. As we raise the anode voltage, anode current increases. At 50 volts it is 4mA, but it has risen to 6mA at 100 volts. If the bias voltage is unchanged, altering the anode potential by 50 volts changes the anode current by 2mA [88]. In Figure 86 changing the grid potential by 1 volt changed the anode current by 2mA. So altering grid potential by 1 volt has the same result on anode current as changing the anode potential by 50 volts.

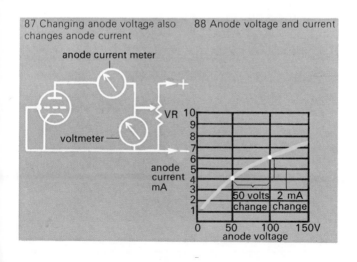

87 Changing anode voltage also changes anode current

88 Anode voltage and current

Triode Amplifier

An audio signal is applied to X in Figure 89. Resistor R1 completes the valve grid circuit. Cathode current flows through R2. We need the control grid to be −2 volts relative to the cathode K. So R2 drops 2 volts. C1 bypasses R2 at frequencies to be amplified.

With no signal at X, bias is −2 volts and anode current is 6mA. The audio signal is 2 volts from peak to peak, so swings the grid from 1 volt to 3 volts. Anode current swings from 8mA to 4mA. The voltage dropped in resistor R3 depends on anode current. So the anode voltage also swings up and down. An amplified signal is taken off by capacitor C2. Such capacitors isolate other circuits [90].

More Electrodes

A screen grid G2 between control grid G1 and anode [91] has a positive potential. Anode current depends less on

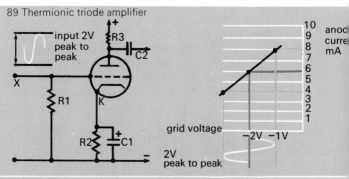

89 Thermionic triode amplifier

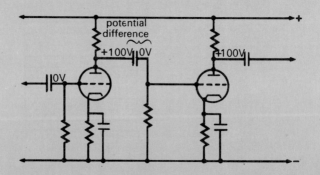

90 Isolating direct current circuits by coupling capacitors

the anode voltage, and amplification is increased. Electrons may be knocked off the anode and return to the positively charged screen grid. The suppressor grid G3 hinders this. This valve is a pentode. Shaped plates between screen grid and anode in a 'beam tetrode' also hinder the flow of electrons from anode to screen grid.

We control the electron stream from two circuits by using a valve with more grids, such as a heptode [92]. Signals applied to grids G1 and G3 control the electron flow.

Grids 2 and 4 form a screen each side of G3. G5 is the suppressor grid.

A double triode has two triodes in a single bulb. A double diode triode has two diodes together with a triode assembly.

In the same way, there are other valves, such as triode-hexodes, triode pentodes, pentodes with diodes, and double pentodes.

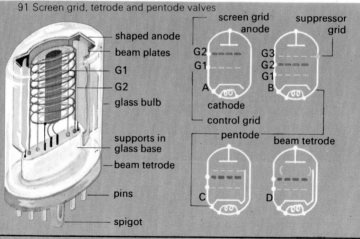

91 Screen grid, tetrode and pentode valves

shaped anode
beam plates
G1
G2
glass bulb
supports in glass base
beam tetrode
pins
spigot

screen grid
anode
G2
G1
A
cathode
control grid

suppressor grid
G3
G2
G1
B

pentode
C

beam tetrode
D

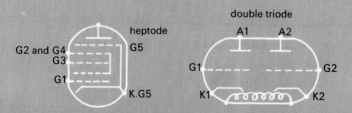

92 Two more multi-electrode valves

heptode
G2 and G4
G3
G1
G5
K.G5

double triode
A1   A2
G1 ---------- G2
K1   K2

Vari-Mu Pentodes

Amplification can be controlled by using a grid having irregular spacing [93]. By increasing the negative bias, the amplification can be reduced to a very small fraction. The valve might have a mutual conductance of 5mA/V with zero bias, falling to 0·005mA/V with 20 volt bias.

Negative Resistance Condition

If a screen grid valve has certain screen grid and anode potentials, electrons strike the anode at a velocity causing

93 Control grid of variable mu valve

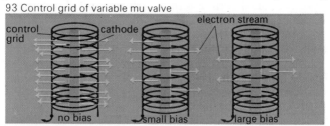

other electrons to be liberated. These 'secondary emission' electrons return to the screen grid. When potentials are suitable, and the screen grid potential is higher than the anode, secondary emission is considerable. If the anode voltage is increased, electrons strike it with added velocity, and liberate more secondary electrons. So over a certain part of the operating curve anode current *falls* for an increase in anode voltage [94]. This is 'negative resistance'. It can cancel the actual or positive resistance of a circuit, sustaining oscillation.

Valve Component Parts

Figure 95 shows parts of a small transmitting valve. Many receiver valves are quite similar in design, though generally

94 Negative resistance screen grid valve

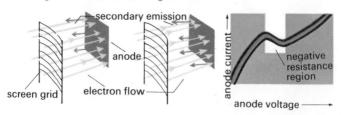

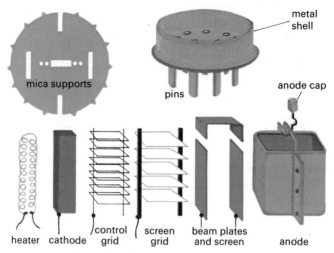

95 A small transmitting valve—component parts

with all connections to base pins. The heater is in the cathode. Then come control grid, screen grid, beam plates and anode. The whole is supported by mica parts pushed inside a glass bulb. As high voltages are present, the anode has a top cap. The insulated base has pins. Smaller valves may be all-glass, with pins in a glass base.

Gas-Filled Thyratron

This contains a gas which ionizes when sufficient current flows, reducing the internal resistance [96]. When the grid is sufficiently negative no electron current flows. Less negative potential causes electrons to flow, ionizing the gas. The valve conducts heavily until the anode potential is reduced.

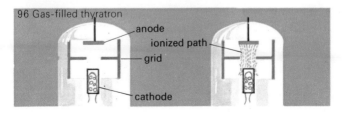

96 Gas-filled thyratron

Semiconductors

The electrons of an atom have various energy levels so that they can be thought of as occupying different bands or positions. Free electrons in the outer position, or shell, can move from atom to atom, forming an electric current.

Germanium has 32 electrons, with four in the outer shell. By adding impurities, an excess or lack of electrons is arranged. Indium has 49 electrons, with three in the outer shell. This is one less than the germanium outer shell, so an electron from a germanium atom can move in to occupy the space, leaving a germanium atom with a deficiency of one electron. This, a positive 'hole', can accept an electron from another germanium atom [97].

Antimony has 51 electrons, with five in the outer shell. This extra electron can displace an adjoining electron, which in turn can move elsewhere.

Lack of an electron leaves a positive charge, so the crystal is termed 'P-type'. Excess of electrons constitutes a negative charge and gives 'N-type' material. Movement of the electrons or hole carriers forms an electric current.

A semiconductor junction diode is a junction of N-type and P-type regions, and is often called a PN diode. Current in N-type germanium is conveyed mostly by electrons, but in the P-type mostly by holes [98].

The diode allows current to pass readily in the 'forward' direction. There are many positive holes to move across to the N-region, and numerous negative electrons to travel to the P-region [99]. This represents a large flow of

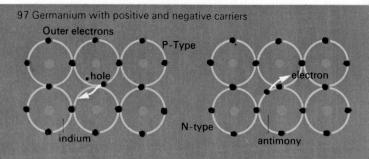

97 Germanium with positive and negative carriers

Outer electrons

P-Type

hole

electron

N-type

indium

antimony

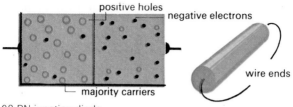

98 PN junction diode

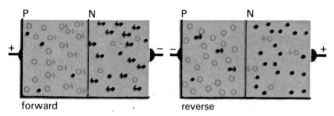

99 Junction with forward and reverse voltage

current across the junction. With the voltage reversed, there are few negative electrons in the P-region, and few positive holes in the N-region, so that the current is small. Semiconductor diodes are made to suit the voltage, current and frequency [100]. Point contact diodes pass small currents, but can operate at very high frequencies.

Germanium rectifiers tend to fail around 75°C, while silicon can withstand up to about 200°C. Thus a silicon rectifier is less affected by rises in temperature, and can operate with currents of many amperes.

100 Some semi-conductor diodes

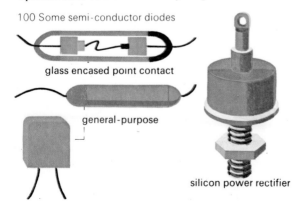

glass encased point contact

general-purpose

silicon power rectifier

Semiconductor diodes are now much used in power supply circuits for rectification. They are small in size, have low forward resistance, can handle high voltages and current, and need no separate heater supply.

Many electronic circuits, including those of receivers and amplifiers, require direct current. The alternating current supply is usually taken to the primary (P) of a mains transformer [101]. This isolates equipment from any actual connection with the mains. Voltage can be reduced or increased by a suitable turns ratio.

The diode allows current to pass readily one way and so can charge a reservoir capacitor. Compare this with the half-wave valve circuit. Semiconductor diodes can also be used in full-wave circuits, to make use of both half-cycles of the AC supply, as with valves.

When rectifiers are working at maximum current, heat is produced. This is carried away by a metal plate or heat sink. Rectifiers may be connected in series or parallel, to obtain a higher voltage or current rating, or they can be stacked in special assemblies [102].

101 Power diode allows DC to be obtained from AC

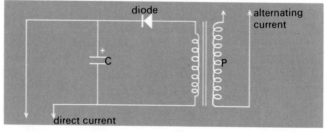

102 Rectifier stack with convection cooling

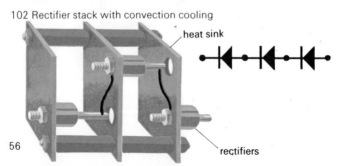

Compensating Diode

In transistor receivers and amplifiers, working conditions of the output transistors which supply the loudspeaker are quite critical. Wrong bias will increase battery drain, or cause distortion.

Base bias which is suitable for a new battery may be unsatisfactory with one that is partly discharged. The temperature at which they are operating affects somewhat the working of transistors.

A compensating diode [103] helps overcome this. The diode's resistance (and transistor operation) varies with the temperature. When battery voltage falls, current through the diode is less. Its resistance rises, helping to shift the base supply more negative and restore satisfactory working.

RF Probe

The point contact diode has extremely small internal capacity, and can operate at very high frequencies. It is suitable for a radio frequency probe [104]. The probe can be taken to any circuit point where RF is present.

103 Diode to stabilize performance

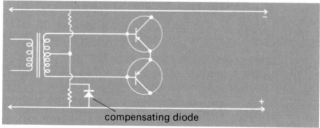

compensating diode

104 Isolated VHF probe

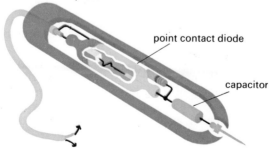

point contact diode

capacitor

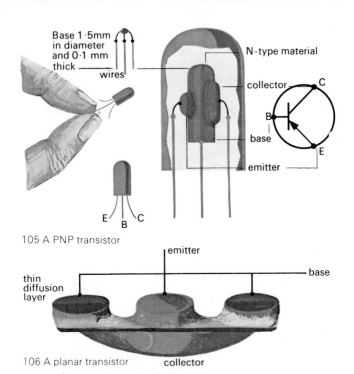

Base 1·5mm in diameter and 0·1 mm thick

wires

N-type material

collector

base

emitter

C

B

E

E B C

105 A PNP transistor

emitter

base

thin diffusion layer

106 A planar transistor   collector

Transistors

A transistor has a central region, or base, of one kind of semiconductor material, with junctions of an opposite kind of material on each side. A PNP transistor has positive-negative-positive material, with a negative central base [105]. The NPN transistor has negative-positive-negative material – a positive central region or base.

For the PNP transistor, pellets of indium are fused on by heating, and diffuse into the base to form P-type regions. The whole is fitted with leads and sealed in a protective case.

Such a transistor becomes less efficient at high frequencies. An alloy junction transistor has a base region only a small fraction of a millimetre wide. Planar transistors [106] made by alloy diffusion have an extremely thin active base region, and construction which reduces the

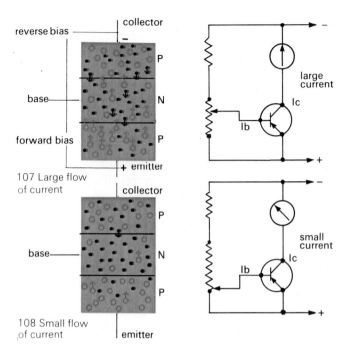

107 Large flow of current

108 Small flow of current

time required for the movement of the current carriers.

The PNP emitter is connected to a positive supply, and the collector to a negative [107]. If the base is appreciably negative, relative to the emitter, the emitter-base junction acts as a diode junction with forward bias. Holes pass into the base, and are drawn by the negative charge of the collector, so that they usually flow to the collector. Current passing through the transistor is large.

If the forward bias is reduced, fewer holes travel to the collector. The current flow is quite small [108]. In a PNP transistor, there is a small movement of 'minority' or negative electron carriers, the 'majority' or most numerous carriers being positive holes – a positive charge equal to an electron. Base and collector currents added together form approximately the emitter current. Almost all the emitter current passes to the collector.

Note the important difference between PNP and NPN transistors [109]. The PNP transistor base is negative type material, and majority current carriers are positive holes, caused by a deficiency of negative electrons. Emitter goes to *positive*. With the NPN transistor, the base is positive type material, and electrons are majority carriers. Emitter goes to *negative*.

Note that the arrow symbol is always the emitter, and agrees with the motion of positive hole carriers. We can regard this as the conventional electrical current flow from positive to negative, encountered in some text books. The flow of electron current is from negative to positive. A heavy current may flow if a supply is connected in the wrong polarity to a transistor. If resistors, etc., do not impede this current, transistor junction may be damaged.

Internal Feedback
The electrodes of a transistor are very close together and this and other effects cause unwanted feedback from the

109 PNP transistor and NPN transistor compared

110 Screened transistor

base
emitter collector
screen

collector. In Figure 110, an imaginary capacitor connection from collector to base stands for the unwanted feedback. This is usually unimportant at low frequencies, but troublesome at high frequencies, where special precautions have to be taken to avoid oscillation or other effects.

Transistors for high frequencies may have a fourth lead, or shield, between base and collector [110]. It helps to reduce unwanted feedback.

Receiver transistors [111] are usually quite small, with insulated or metal cases.

They are made for radio frequency amplification, audio amplification, etc. They are also produced in small sizes for miniature equipment.

Power transistors [112] for RF and audio amplification are larger; usually they can be clamped to a metal plate or heat sink, to help avoid overheating. Some transistors are made in similar or matched pairs, in a single case. Other transistors are intended for computer 'logic' and various special applications.

111 Small receiver and amplifier transistors

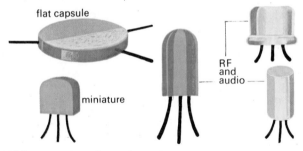

flat capsule

miniature

RF and audio

112 Power and matched pair transistors

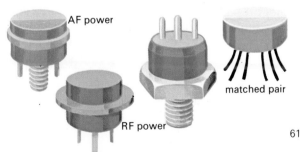

AF power

RF power

matched pair

Some Circuit Points

We use transistors in various ways. Some are shown in Figure 113. Here A has input to emitter and base, with output from collector and base. R is a load resistor across which power is developed, or a tuning coil or other device. Both input and output circuits use the base, so A is a *common and grounded base* arrangement.

B has input between base and emitter, and output developed across collector and emitter circuits. It is a *common and grounded emitter*. In the same way C is a *common emitter grounded collector* arrangement.

A, B and C are NPN transistors. D is a PNP transistor with input to base and emitter, and output developed across collector and emitter circuits. It is a *common emitter grounded emitter* circuit.

Some methods provide best power gain. Others operate better at high frequency. Some have high impedance input and low impedance output, or the reverse. The 'impedance' is the 'resistance' at working frequency. Figure 114 shows the transistor as a current generator, with input impedance R1 and output impedance R2. Maximum useful power results when input and output circuits match R1 and R2.

Dynamic Working

Figure 115 is a PNP common emitter amplifier, with base bias set by R1 and R2 and output developed across R3. C1 and C2 isolate the stage from other direct current points. R4 provides emitter bias to stabilize working, and has a by-pass capacitor, C3.

Base current Ib is at some small steady value. Collector current Ic is also at a steady value, and emitter current Ie approximately equals Ib plus Ic. Currents are indicated without regard to polarity. When a signal to be amplified arrives through C1, base current swings up and down with each cycle, as shown in [116-Ib]. Slight increases in base current cause large increases in emitter-collector current. So collector current Ic swings up and down in value, developing an output voltage across R3.

A moving-coil meter would show the average currents [115], an oscilloscope dynamic conditions.

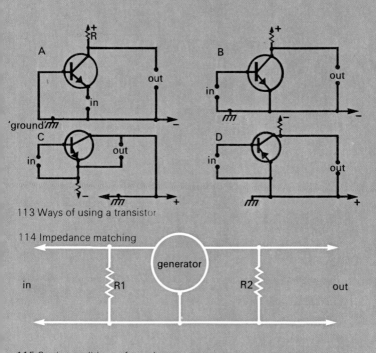

113 Ways of using a transistor

114 Impedance matching

115 Static conditions of transistor

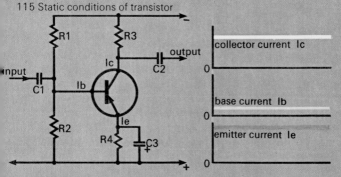

116 Dynamic working during amplification

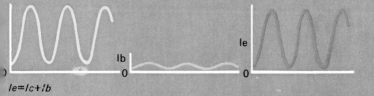

$Ie = Ic + Ib$

AUDIO, RADIO, TV, TAPES

Audio Amplifiers

A signal is 'amplified' to make it stronger. An audio amplifier deals with frequencies from about 15 Hz to 15,000 Hz. Musical items mostly lie in the 50 Hz to 2,000 Hz range, but 'harmonics' must be reproduced for good results. The electrical output of a record-player pick-up may be a few millivolts. A loudspeaker needs much more power, so signals are amplified [117].

Figure 118 is a triode valve audio amplifier. There is 2 volts negative bias through R1 for the control grid. The valve passes 1mA from its cathode to its anode. Anode current flows through R2. From Ohm's Law ($V = I \times R$) the voltage lost in R2 is 100 volts. Suppose a positive

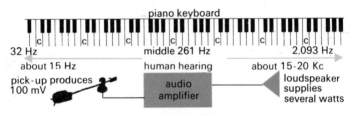

117 Audio spectrum and need for amplification

signal peak of 1 volt reaches the grid [119a]. The grid voltage is now −1 volt. Anode current rises to 1·5mA. So 1·5mA flows through R2. The voltage drop is now 150 volts, leaving 50 volts at the anode. Imagine that a 1 volt negative peak reaches the grid, B. This adds to the −2 volts present, giving −3 volts. Suppose anode current falls to 0·5mA. The voltage lost in R2 is now 50 volts, so the anode potential is $200 - 50 = 150$ volts.

Hence by applying a signal which swings 1 volt above and below zero we have obtained an output or anode voltage which swings from 150 volts to 50 volts.

C1 is the usual coupling capacitor [120]. It interrupts any direct current path, but it has little reactance at audio frequency, and therefore lets signals pass. In the same way, C2 feeds another stage.

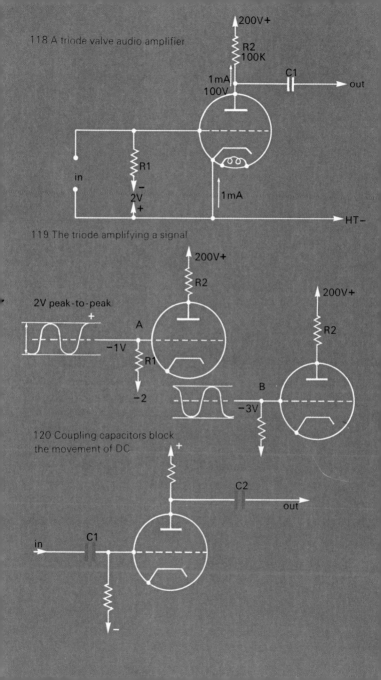

118 A triode valve audio amplifier

200V+

R2
100K

1mA
100V

C1
out

R1

in

−
2V
+

1mA

HT−

119 The triode amplifying a signal

200V+

R2

2V peak-to-peak

+

A

−1V

R1

−2

200V+

R2

B

−3V

120 Coupling capacitors block
the movement of DC

+

C2
out

in   C1

−

We need the control grid to receive a small negative bias voltage. Figure 121 has cathode bias resistor R3, which must drop 2 volts with 1mA passing. $\frac{V}{I} = R$. So R3 is 2,000 ohms.

C3 across R3 'by-passes' the cathode to earth at working frequency. We often use a pentode and get higher 'gain' or amplification than from a triode [122]. VR is a potentiometer which allows any portion of the signal voltage to be taken, and so acts as volume control. RS supplies the screen grid G2, and CS is the screen grid by-pass capacitor. The suppressor grid is at the same potential as the cathode.

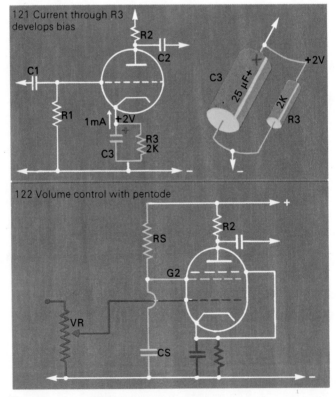

121 Current through R3 develops bias

122 Volume control with pentode

Useful work is done by the anode load resistor R2 – a signal voltage is developed across it. The valve, with resistors and other components, is termed a 'stage'. The 'stage gain' or amplification achieved is less than the amplification factor of the valve.

Imaginary resistor Ra [123a] represents the valve internal impedance and the anode load resistor R2 is chosen to suit this. With output valves this is termed the 'optimum' (best) load. In Figure 123b it is furnished by the transformer and speaker. By choosing a suitable transformer ratio, we can provide any optimum load we choose.

Loudspeaker impedance will often be about 2 to 15 ohms. Transformer ratio is usually from about 15:1 to 60:1.

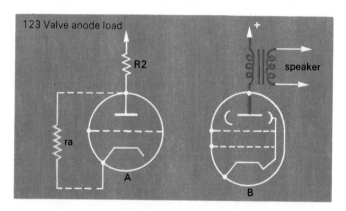

123 Valve anode load

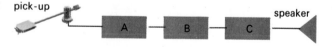

124 Three-stage amplifier

Cascaded Stages

We usually need more amplification than is provided by one stage, so use two or more stages [124]. Here A could be an initial voltage amplifier [122], B a further amplifier stage [121], and C an output stage working a loudspeaker.

Transformer Coupling

In Figure 125 the transformer primary winding receives audio signals from an earlier stage. The secondary delivers signals to the next grid. This system is little used today, but the diagram will help to explain circuits given later. When one end of the secondary swings negative, the other end is positive. For the next half-cycle, this is reversed.

Figure 126 has a centre-tapped secondary. For one half-cycle V1 receives a negative signal, but V2 a positive signal. So V1 passes less anode current, and V2 more anode current. During the next half-cycle the opposite arises so that V1 current increases and V2 current falls.

The 'half outputs' from V1 and V2 go to the output transformer primary. They are combined and work the speaker, connected to secondary S. This is called 'push-pull'. We can also provide so much bias that anode current is nearly cut off except when a valve grid receives a positive signal voltage. This is called 'Class B' operation, and saves HT current.

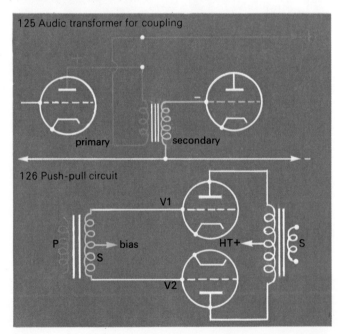

125 Audio transformer for coupling

primary   secondary

126 Push-pull circuit

V1

P   bias   HT+   S

S

V2

Resistance Capacity Coupling can be employed instead. In Figure 127, V1 receives audio signals at G1. When its anode current rises, the voltage drop in R1 and R2 increases. So point X swings negative, and Y swings positive. The result is like using a centre-tapped transformer to supply V2 and V3. Signals go via C1 and C2. R3 and R4 are grid resistors. R5 supplies cathode bias.

Negative Feedback

We can take part of the output signal and return it to *oppose* the original signal. This reduces distortion. Components such as capacitors have varying effects as frequency changes. Suppose the amplifier gives most amplification to high tones, or has too much 'top'. If we feed back signals to oppose the input, these top frequencies will be most strongly present. This will reduce high frequencies more than lower frequencies. The overall result is better 'fidelity', or faithfulness of amplification. In Figure 128, feedback is through R1 to the valve cathode.

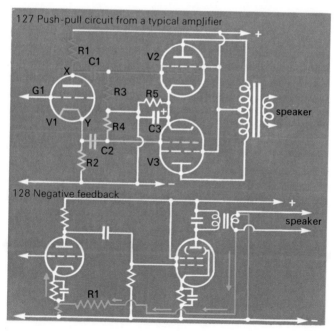

127 Push-pull circuit from a typical amplifier

128 Negative feedback

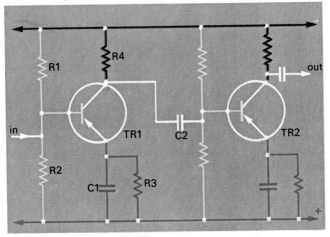

Transistor Audio Amplifier

Figure 129 has TR1 as audio amplifier. R1 and R2 are chosen so that a small base current flows and the PNP transistor base is slightly more negative than the emitter. R3 stabilizes the working conditions by emitter bias. If current rises, more voltage is lost in R3. So the emitter is more negative. This lowers the base-to-emitter voltage and reduces current. C1 by-passes R3 at working frequency.

Changes in base current from the signal source cause changes in collector current. These develop a signal voltage across the load resistor R4. C2 has low reactance at audio frequencies, so signals arrive at the base of the second transistor TR2. Because of C2 the circuit is called 'capacitor coupled'. TR2 gives further amplification.

In Figure 130, potentials on TR1 collector and TR2 base are arranged to be the same, so that they can be directly connected. This is 'direct coupling'.

Figure 131 has three stages of amplification, all directly coupled. The collector voltages on TR1 and TR2 will be low, but can be sufficient for good results.

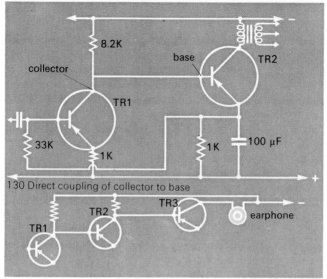

130 Direct coupling of collector to base

131 Direct coupling for miniature deaf aid

Car Radio

Figure 132 is a typical car radio amplifier. The output transistor needs a large current, but can work directly from a 12 volt accumulator. Only one transistor is present. It must amplify the whole audio cycle. This is termed Class A operation.

Speaker matching is by a tapped winding, instead of a transformer with separate primary and secondary. Such a tapped component is an 'auto-transformer'.

132 Car radio Class A ouput stage

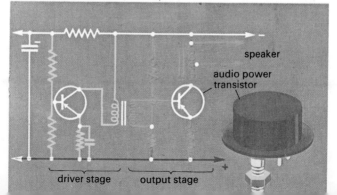

Push-Pull Too

'Class B' working with transistors uses base bias which causes collector current to be lower than with 'Class A'. Figure 133 has resistors R1 and R2 to supply the bases of TR1 and TR2 through the transformer secondary. When audio signals drive TR1 into the conducting region for one half-cycle, collector current rises. For the other half-cycle TR2 is made to conduct [134]. This is analogous to the use of thermionic valves in push-pull. Battery drain is small at low volume, or when no signal is present, but rises to allow adequate loudspeaker volume when required.

Figure 135 shows an arrangement often found in miniature transistor receivers. The transformer has two secondaries, each driving one transistor. The transistors conduct on alternate halves of the signal cycle. No output transformer is needed, and a miniature 75 ohm or other speaker can be fed directly.

Stereophonic Amplifier

A stereo amplifier [136] has two channels. Volume control VR1 takes off the required signal level from a stereo pick-

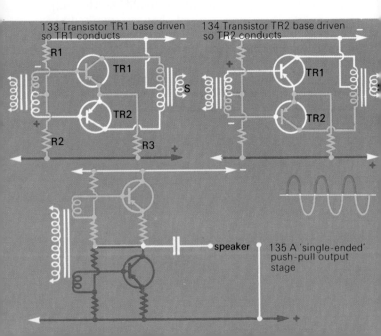

133 Transistor TR1 base driven so TR1 conducts

134 Transistor TR2 base driven so TR2 conducts

135 A 'single-ended' push-pull output stage

up, which supplies right-hand and left-hand outputs. Signals pass through R1 and R2 to V1A. V1A and V1B are assemblies of a triode-tetrode. R4 is the anode load, and C3 couples to the control grid of V1B. R5 and R8 with by-pass capacitors C2 and C5 provide cathode bias. R7 and C4 drop and smooth the HT supply for V1A. Transformer T couples to the speaker. Higher frequencies pass back through C6 and R9 to the junction of R2 and R3, to provide selective feedback controlled by VR2, for adjusting treble.

The left-hand channel output of the pick-up goes to a second identical amplifier, and to the left-hand speaker. A common power pack supplies both amplifiers, and the equipment is generally assembled on a single chassis.

During the recording, right- and left-hand channels depend on strength according to the position of the musical instruments or performers, and so a person listening to the speakers in Figure 136 obtains a sensation of depth. (See also page 104.) A similar effect is obtained when listening to stereo broadcasts. Special means are used to provide right- and left-hand channels.

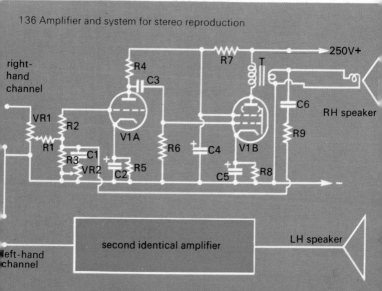

136 Amplifier and system for stereo reproduction

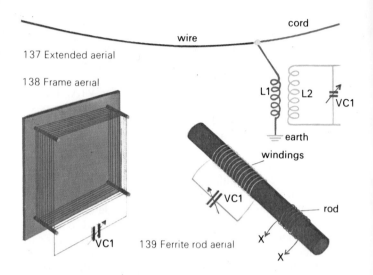

137 Extended aerial

138 Frame aerial

139 Ferrite rod aerial

How a Radio Receiver Works

Radio waves travel 300,000,000 metres a second, with the electromagnetic field and the electrostatic field at right angles. We speak of 'wavelength' or 'frequency'. If the wave changes from positive to negative and back 300,000 times a second, there will be 1,000 metres from the crest of one wave to the next. So a wavelength of 1,000 metres equals a frequency of 300,000 cycles per second (hertz).

1,000 hertz = 1 kilocycle, 1kHz, or 1 kilo hertz

1,000m = 300kHz

1,000kHz = 1 megacycle, 1Mc/s, or 1MHz.

An extended wire can intercept part of the radio wave [137]. A signal voltage across the coil L1 induces a voltage in the coil L2, which is tuned by the variable capacitor VC1 to select the desired frequency.

Portable receivers may use a frame aerial [138]. The wave induces a signal voltage in the winding, which is tuned to the desired station by VC1. Small portables generally have a ferrite rod aerial [139]. A winding is tuned by VC1. A smaller coupling winding X-X supplies a

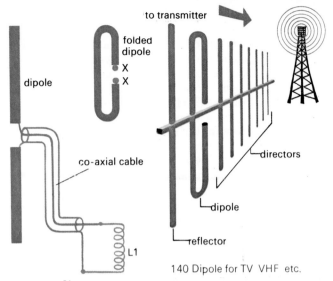

140 Dipole for TV VHF etc.

transistor. Frame and ferrite rod aerials are directive. They pick up signals best when an imaginary axis through the windings is at right angles to the direction of the transmitter. Pick-up is least when the axis points to the transmitter. This is used in direction-finding equipment. (See also page 122.)

TV and VHF

TV and VHF ('very high frequency') transmissions are of very short wavelength, and so a dipole can be used [140]. It is about the same length as a half-wave. It is cut at the centre and a 75 ohm co-axial or twin feeder connected. This carries signal currents to the coil L1.

A slightly longer element or 'reflector' can be put behind the dipole. This increases signal strength. Shorter elements or 'directors' may be positioned in front of the dipole. The elements may be arranged like an H, or an X.

Adding a reflector and directors changes the centre impedance of the dipole, making it low. Therefore it is folded and the feeder is attached to X-X. The aerial has its elements placed vertically and horizontally to match the 'polarization' of the TV or VHF signal.

Resonance

Radio transmitters use different frequencies. To choose a signal we tune a circuit to 'resonance' with it. Figure 141 is a parallel-tuned circuit. The 'resonant frequency' is that at which a signal voltage is developed across the coil. Altering the capacity VC1 changes the resonant frequency. VC1 is operated by a drive having a dial marked with frequencies, stations, or wavelengths.

With a fixed coil L1, moving VC1 from minimum to maximum capacity covers a range of frequencies, or 'waveband'. One band is about 1,500kc to 600kc, or 200 to 500 metres (medium waves). For other wavebands, we select coils of different size and inductance. Figure 142 has S1 to select L1 or L2. Other coils can be present.

Often the coils have other windings, such as the coupling primaries. Then section S2 can choose these at the same time. A receiver may have several coils and a switch with a number of sections.

We may tune two or more circuits at once. Figure 143 has the aerial coil with primary P1 and secondary

141 Parallel tuned current

142 Selecting different wavebands

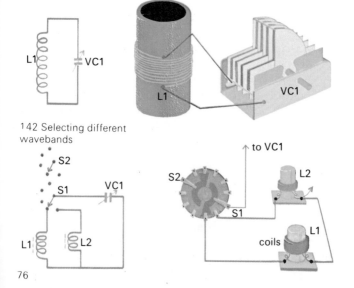

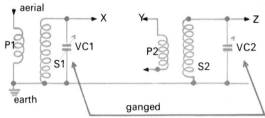

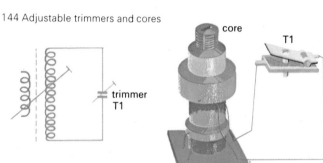

S1, tuned by VC1. Amplified signals go to Y and to the primary P2. The secondary S2 is tuned by VC2. The ganged capacitor VC1–VC2 has two sets of plates with a single spindle. In some receivers, VC1 and VC2 both tune the same frequency – that of the transmission wanted. Two tuned circuits make the receiver more 'selective': we can better choose or select one station from others on near frequencies.

In superhet receivers, VC2 tunes to a different frequency. By a process called 'frequency changing' all stations produce a signal of the same frequency. Later circuits can be permanently tuned to this new frequency.

Often each coil has an adjustable core [144]. Its inductance can be matched with other coils. Coils generally have a trimmer T1. This compensates for stray circuit capacity in wiring, valves, transistors, etc. The service engineer adjusts cores and trimmers so that the circuits 'gang' as exactly as possible together.

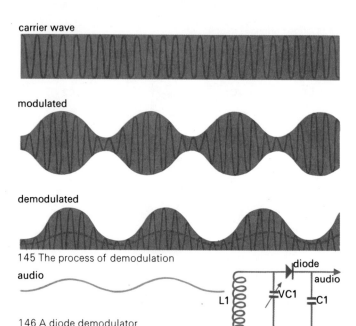

carrier wave

modulated

demodulated

145 The process of demodulation

audio

146 A diode demodulator

Demodulation

Putting the audible programme into the radio wave is called 'modulation'. Recovering the sound from the signal is 'demodulation' or 'detection'. A radio wave with no modulation is of uniform strength [145]. Many broadcasts use 'amplitude' modulation. A radio wave modulated with a single tone is represented, but for speech and music the shape is very complicated. The modulated wave reaches a diode in the receiver. This lets current pass one way only, and so removes one-half of the modulated waves, as shown in the diagram.

The peaks of the radio signals are smoothed by later circuits, leaving a copy of the audio signal used to modulate the transmitted signal. In Figure 146 L1 is tuned to the desired station by VC1. Signal voltages resemble the 'modulated' wave. The diode produces the 'demodulated' wave. Capacitor C1 helps smooth the radio frequency peaks to produce the audio output. This could be heard with headphones, but as a rule will pass to an amplifier. When the signals are strong, enough output is obtained from the diode to work headphones [147]. This is the simple crystal diode receiver, similar in performance to the crystal sets so popular in the early days of radio. Semiconductor diodes were not then made, but an efficient detector consisted of a crystal, and cat's-whisker of thin wire. This resembled the point contact diode.

In valve receivers, a thermionic diode often provides demodulation. The heated cathode emits electrons, and the diode conducts from cathode to anode only [148]. The audio signal is developed across R1, and taken from C2 to an amplifier. L1 is usually the secondary of an 'intermediate frequency transformer'. The diode is generally part of a diode-triode or double-diode-triode valve. The triode section is used for audio amplification. C1 is a radio frequency by-pass capacitor.

Nearly all receivers are 'superhets' – abbreviated from 'supersonic-heterodyne'. In a superhet, an oscillator

147 A crystal diode receiver

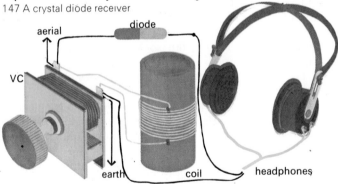

148 Thermionic valve diode as demodulator

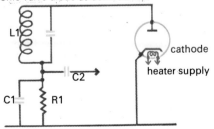

generates a signal which is made to beat with, or heterodyne, signals tuned in. This produces a fixed frequency, which passes to an amplifier with fixed tuned circuits. The frequencies are above audibility.

In Figure 149 the station desired is tuned in by L1 and VC1. L2 is an oscillator coil, tuned by VC2. If two frequencies are mixed, another frequency produced is equal to the difference. Suppose L1 is tuned to 200kHz and L2 to 670kHz. The difference is 470kHz. Should L1 be adjusted to 1,400kHz, and L2 to 1,870kHz, the difference is still 470kHz. By arranging that the *difference* between L1 and L2 frequencies remains unchanged, the same frequency output is obtained.

Figure 150 is a transistor frequency changer. L1 is tuned to the desired transmission. L2 transfers the signals to the base B. L3 is the oscillator coil, with windings connected to collector C and emitter E. R3 is for emitter bias.

If L1 tunes from 500kHz to 1,500kHz for medium waves, and the later stages are to operate at 470kHz, then L3 tunes from 970kHz to 1,970kHz. The *ratio* of frequencies covered by L3 (970:1,970) is smaller than frequencies covered by L1 (500:1,500) so VC2 is smaller, or has a capacitor C in series.

The desired frequency from the frequency changer is the intermediate frequency'. It is often around 455kHz to 470kHz, but much higher in receivers for high frequencies.

Switching can select other coils, for more wavebands [151]. Each coil can have its own trimmer and adjustable core.

Some receivers have a radio frequency amplifier before the frequency changer [152]. This is tuned to the desired station frequency ('signal frequency'). Valve receivers operate in a similar way, with the circuit arranged for valves.

When signals have been converted to a chosen fixed frequency, they pass to the 'intermediate frequency' amplifier. Signals have been converted from radio frequency to this intermediate frequency. Later they will become a lower, audio frequency.

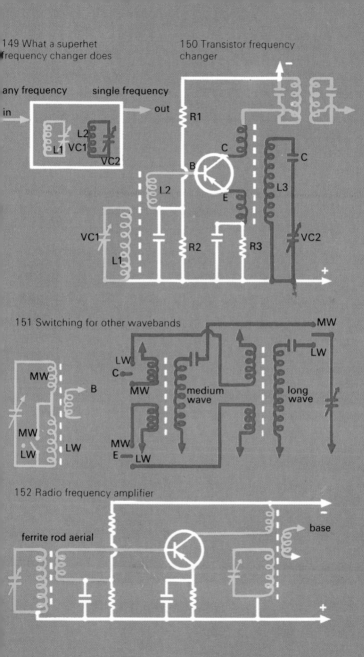

149 What a superhet frequency changer does

any frequency
in

single frequency
out

L1 L2 VC1 VC2

150 Transistor frequency changer

R1

B C E

VC1 L1 L2 R2 R3 L3 C VC2

151 Switching for other wavebands

MW
B
MW
LW

LW
C
MW

MW
E LW

MW
medium wave
long wave

MW
LW

152 Radio frequency amplifier

ferrite rod aerial

base

IF Amplifier

The intermediate frequency transformer IFT1 [153] is permanently tuned to the intermediate frequency. After amplification by transistor TR1, signals pass to IFT2, then to transistor TR2. Each transistor has base supplies at X and Y. IFT3 feeds the demodulator diode D1. Audio signals are obtained across the volume control VR1. The sliding contact takes off audio signals as required.

Transformers, used to couple valves, transistors, or

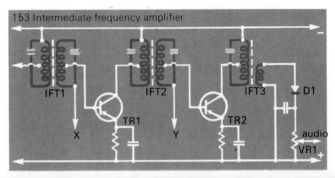

153 Intermediate frequency amplifier

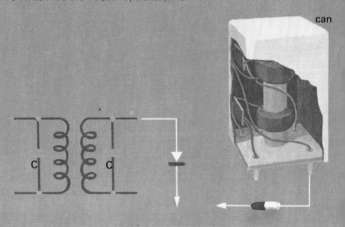

154 Intermediate frequency transformer

other circuits, generally have two windings [154]. Each is permanently tuned by a fixed capacitor C. The cores are screwed in or out, allowing changes in inductance and precise adjustment to the correct frequency. Often the diode winding is not tuned [IFT3, Figure 153]. In some receivers, none of the secondaries is tuned.

A transistor can provide demodulation [155]. Audio signals are taken off through capacitor C. Thermionic diodes, triodes, and other valves can be used as detectors. A semiconductor diode is very popular.

Figure 156 shows the stages of a receiver. The frequency changer converts all incoming signals to one frequency. The intermediate frequency amplifier tuned circuits help eliminate possible interference from other transmissions, and also raise the signal strength. The detector recovers the audio signal. But this is not yet strong enough to operate a loudspeaker and it is raised in level by the audio amplifier. The output stage or last amplifier increases the power even more, and signal strength becomes great enough to drive the loudspeaker. The same sequence of stages is often used in a valve receiver.

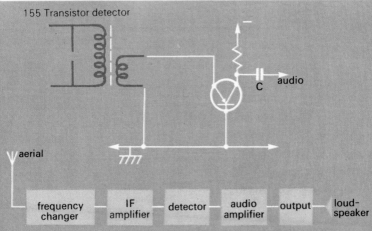

155 Transistor detector

156 Block diagram of a superhet receiver

How a TV Receiver Works

The television station transmits two signals – one for sound and one for vision. It would be possible to use separate receivers and aerials, one for sound and the other for picture reception [157].

But sound and vision frequencies are near each other, so we may employ the same aerial. We can also build the equipment as a single receiver, and employ some sections for both sound and vision [158]. A radio frequency amplifier increases the strength of both sound and vision signals, which are then separated. A common power pack provides current for both sound and vision sections.

TV Sound

The sound programme may be provided by amplitude modulation of the carrier wave. The apparent strength of the wave changes with the audio signals – speech or music, etc. A detector recovers the sound, as with radio.

Sound can also be provided by frequency modulation.

157 Television—sound and vision

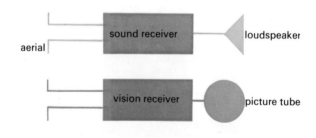

158 Circuits combined in a TV receiver

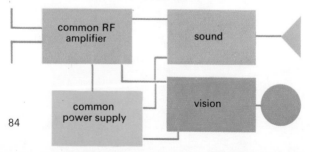

159 Some TV channels showing adjacent sound and vision frequencies

Megacycles

Channel 1	{ 41·54 Sound { 45·00 Vision
Channel 2	{ 48·25 Sound { 51·75 Vision
Channel 3	{ 53·25 Sound { 56·75 Vision
Channel 10	{ 196·25 Sound { 199·75 Vision
Channel 11	{ 201·25 Sound { 204·75 Vision

160 Aerials are made for the channels required, etc.

channel 1

channel 10

vertical polarization

horizontal polarization

The amplitude of the wave remains the same, but its frequency is changed to carry audio signals. The sound is recovered by a 'ratio detector' or other frequency modulation detector.

Each system is used in sound-radio and for TV sound, depending on 'channel' or station.

Frequencies

The frequency or wavelength determines the channel, just as in sound broadcasting [159]. As already mentioned, each station has two adjacent frequencies – one for sound, and one for vision. We usually select the station by some form of rotary or other preset tuning arrangement, to which a variable fine tuner may be added.

The aerial is arranged to suit the channel we want, or we may have a combined aerial for two or more frequencies. The receiver aerial elements must be vertical, or horizontal, in order to suit the 'polarization' of the signals [160], depending on the transmitter.

Figure 161 shows circuits we can use for sound reception. The radio frequency amplifier passes signals to the frequency changer. This fulfils the same purpose as in a radio receiver, and converts signals to the intermediate frequency, to be handled by an IF amplifier of fixed tuning. The IF amplifier first stage is common to both sound and vision circuits. The outputs of this amplifier are separated. Sound signals pass to a further IF amplifier, used for sound only, then to a demodulator or detector, audio amplifier, output stage and loudspeaker.

161 Circuits in use for sound-reception

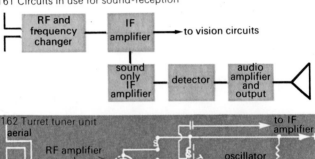

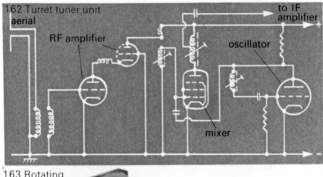

162 Turret tuner unit

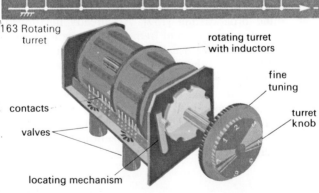

163 Rotating turret

We probably want to receive signals from two widely separated channels. For some changes in frequency we can switch different coils or inductances into circuit. Figure 162 shows a VHF tuner circuit. It has a radio frequency amplifier, followed by a frequency changer and covers a number of frequencies by switching inductors.

The tuner has a turret [163] with a number of inductances set round a shaft. Any of the inductors can be brought into circuit by rotating a control knob. This has a similar effect to the bandswitching seen in radio receivers, but is more efficient.

For ultra high frequencies (UHF) switching is too inefficient: VHF and UHF tuners are used. The VHF tuner, with its own aerial, accepts signals from the desired station in this band. The UHF tuner operates with its own aerial, and selects the higher frequency transmissions.

Signals from either tuner can be passed on to the intermediate frequency amplifier.

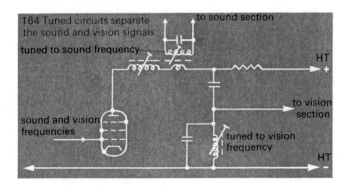

164 Tuned circuits separate the sound and vision signals
tuned to sound frequency
to sound section
HT +
sound and vision frequencies
to vision section
tuned to vision frequency
HT −

Separator
Figure 164 is a combined sound and vision amplifier. Sound signals are separated from vision signals by the transformer. This separation is possible because the sound and vision signals are on different frequencies. Both were mixed with a single common frequency in the oscillator. So the output from the mixer is one frequency for sound, and another for vision.

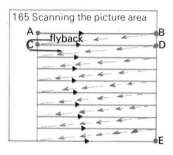

165 Scanning the picture area

Forming a Picture

The picture is formed by a spot of light moving over the tube screen, and increasing or reducing in intensity to make light and dark areas. Covering the screen face in regular lines is called 'scanning'.

In Figure 165 we scan the picture area by starting the spot at A and moving it to B, then flashing it back instantly to C, and moving it along again to D. This is continued until we end at E. From here, the spot returns to A, to begin again.

If we use many lines they lie closely one above the other. By controlling the spot brightness, and covering the whole area many times a second [166], we build up a complete picture.

The TV receiver screen is fluorescent, glowing under the influence of the cathode ray. There is only

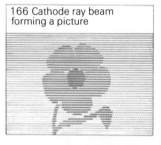

166 Cathode ray beam forming a picture

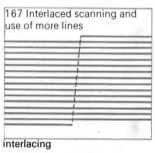

167 Interlaced scanning and use of more lines

interlacing

many lines

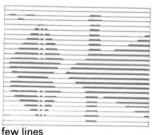

few lines

one small area where the cathode ray strikes the screen at any instant. Persistence of the tube coating, which glows for a short time after the spot has passed, and of vision, make the whole screen appear to be illuminated.

Interlaced scanning of alternate lines is used, as this avoids flickering [167].

It is important that there should be a large number of lines.

If there are few lines the spot area is large and the picture cannot have much detail. A picture made from 405 line signals has less detail than one from a 625 line signal (exaggerated in Figure 167). Some of the line periods are employed for synchronization.

With interlaced scanning, the whole picture area is covered by half the total number of lines. This is a 'frame' and occupies $\frac{1}{50}$ second. The remaining lines cover the screen, filling the spaces between those in the first frame during another $\frac{1}{50}$ second. The process is thus completed in $\frac{1}{25}$ second.

To obtain a picture, the movement of the spot must agree with that of the scanning beam in the camera supplying picture signals. This is arranged by synchronizing pulses [168].

The TV receiver circuits are adjusted for approximately the correct scanning speed. At the end of each line a line synchronizing pulse occurs, and triggers the receiver line-scan circuit. At the end of the frame, a series of pulses triggers the frame-scanning circuit, returning the spot to the beginning of its travel over the picture area.

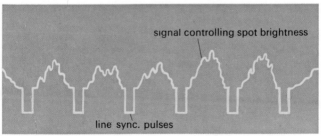

signal controlling spot brightness

line sync. pulses

168 Synchronization of scanning signal controlling spot brightness

How the Scan is Produced

The cathode ray tube cathode emits electrons focused into a narrow beam. This strikes the tube face, causing fluorescence. Magnetic deflection is by coils [169]. Current in two coils deflects the spot from side to side. Current in the other coils moves the spot up or down. They are 'line' and 'frame' scan coils according to purpose.

A rapid sawtooth wave [170] produces line scanning. Rise X causes deflection of the spot. It traces a line across the screen. Flyback (return) of the spot Y to a new line is fast. Voltage rises again after each flyback.

For frame scanning, a slower sawtooth is needed (not shown to scale in Figure 170). Z1 carries the spot smoothly down the screen. After about half the total number of lines, the bottom is reached. The spot flies up to the top, due to the abrupt change Y1. It descends smoothly again during Z2, and returns to the top again during Y2.

169 Pairs of coils used to scan picture area

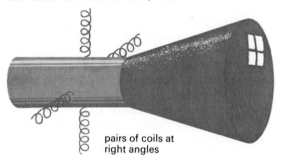

pairs of coils at
right angles

170 Line scan and frame scan waves

line

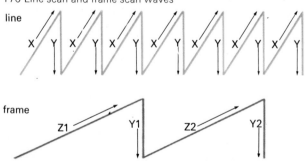

X Y X Y X Y X Y X Y X Y X Y

frame

Z1   Y1   Z2   Y2

Vision Signals

The vision signal goes to the vision IF amplifier, and is increased in strength [171]. Various parts of the signal have to perform specific functions.

Line synchronizing pulses present with the signal synchronize the line oscillator as described, so each line begins at the correct instant. Frame pulses synchronize the frame generator.

Vision signals control the intensity of the spot during its motion, to build up the picture light and shade. The vision or video detector may be a semiconductor diode [172]. Its output passes to an amplifier. The video signal then controls the intensity of the beam, and thus the brilliance of the spot as it travels over the screen.

Figure 173 is a frame oscillator to generate the sawtooth output which deflects the spot. We adjust the oscillator frequency with the frame hold control. If the frequency

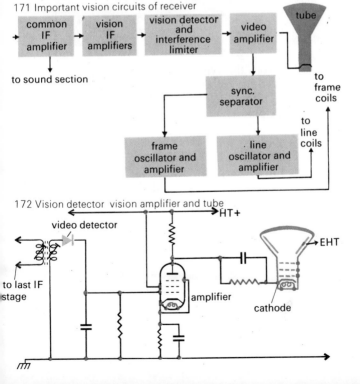

171 Important vision circuits of receiver

172 Vision detector vision amplifier and tube

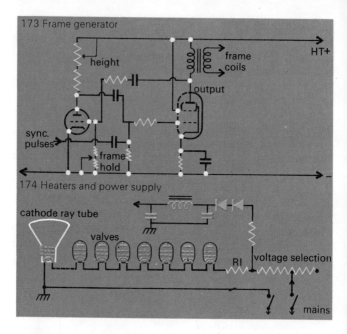

173 Frame generator

174 Heaters and power supply

is too far from the sync pulses, these cannot control the scanning, and the picture breaks up. The frequency of the line scan is also adjusted until it can be synchronized by the line sync pulses.

Power Supplies

TV receivers have many valves, so the heaters are usually connected in series [174]. The voltage needed is the total of all valves added together, and is made up to the mains voltage by resistor R1. Another tapped resistor allows adjustment for 200 volt to 250 volt supplies. This is economical with a large number of valves, but the chassis is alive to the mains.

High tension for most stages of the receiver is obtained with a valve or other rectifier giving 200 volts or so.

The cathode ray tube requires an extra high tension supply of some kilovolts obtained from the line scan circuit [175].

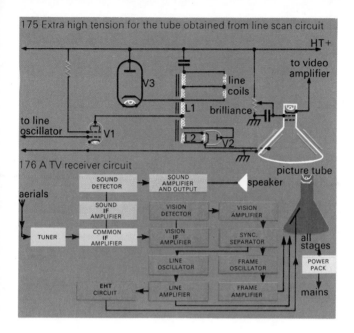

175 Extra high tension for the tube obtained from line scan circuit

176 A TV receiver circuit

V1 is the line output valve, and the tapped winding L1 supplies current to the line coils, to deflect the cathode ray. During flyback, a high e.m.f. is produced in this winding, for the EHT rectifier V2. Current from the small winding L2 heats this valve.

Output from V2 may be smoothed by a high voltage capacitor. Or the tube can have inner and outer coatings, separated by glass and acting as a capacitor. Rectification in V3 boosts the supply; hence the voltage at V1 anode is higher than the HT supply.

Essential sections of a TV receiver are in Figure 176. The tuner selects the station and converts to the intermediate frequency. IF, detector, audio and output stages provide sound. The vision intermediate frequency amplifier, detector and amplifier control the strength of the cathode ray. Pulses synchronize line and frame oscillators, whose outputs go to the deflection coils. Extra high tension is from the line amplifier, HT from a power pack.

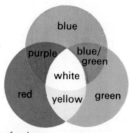

177 Additive mixing of colours

178 A method of obtaining colour signals for transmission

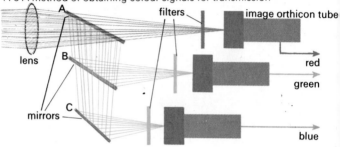

Colour TV

Other colours than black can be made up by mixing three chosen colours. The additive combination of light differs from results obtained with pigments. Absence of all colours forms black. Red and green together provide yellow. Blue and red give purple, and blue and green provide blue-green [177]. When red, blue and green are present in an intensity of 40%, 26% and 34%, combining them provides white.

To transmit a colour picture, the scene is scanned by cameras sensitive to three colours, which are reproduced in the receiver. Other colours are reproduced by changing the intensity of the red, blue and green channels.

Figure 178 is a colour camera system. Mirror A lets red pass, but reflects blue and green. B reflects green but transmits blue, which is reflected by C. In this way the scene scanned is separated into the three colours, each providing its own signal. Other arrangements of selective mirrors may be used in order to obtain the desired result. The picture could be reproduced by three projection tubes, one each for red, green and blue, and each receiving the red, green or blue signal [179].

A shadow mask colour tube has three separate cathode assemblies [180]. Each emits a ray controlled by the red, green or blue channels. A mask with many small holes is fitted inside the tube. The cathode rays come from slightly different directions, and after passing through the same hole strike different spots on the screen. The screen is coated so that rays from the blue channel gun strike areas producing blue. The cathode ray responsible for green strikes areas which produce green, and in the same way the red-producing ray strikes areas which cause red. The different colour spots are so small that the eye blends them together into the various hues wanted. Deflection coils move the three cathode rays over the tube face together.

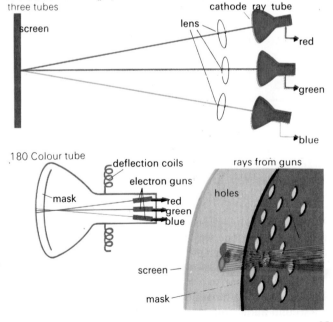

179 Colour receiving system with three tubes

screen

lens

cathode ray tube

red

green

blue

180 Colour tube

deflection coils

electron guns

mask

red
green
blue

rays from guns

holes

screen

mask

Recording on Tape, and Disc Stereo

Tape recordings are much used for video or television picture recording, input and storage of computer information, and other purposes.

For sound recording, the signal level is raised with an audio amplifier [181], and taken to a recording head. This has a winding and magnetic material core with a narrow gap. Signals in the winding cause a fluctuating magnetic field across this gap.

The tape is polyvinyl chloride or other insulating material, coated on one side with tiny particles of ferrous oxide. It is often $\frac{1}{4}$ in. wide for sound, and 2 in. for video.

181 Amplification and recording head

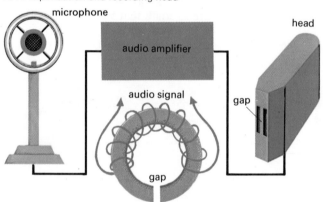

The unused tape has magnetic particles lying at random [182]. A mechanism draws the tape smoothly by the head gap. The particles are brought into magnetic alignment, and the tape has magnetized areas corresponding to the audio currents in the head winding.

For longer playing time, about half the track is used with the tape passing one way, and the remaining half with the tape reversed. Quarter-track recording is also used.

Frequency Response

Suppose the tape moves 15 in. per second and a 15 cycle per second audio tone is recorded. There will be 1 in. tape

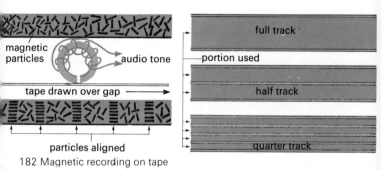

182 Magnetic recording on tape

length from one cycle peak to the next. If the tape moves at $7\frac{1}{2}$ ips the distance would fall to $\frac{1}{2}$ in. For slower tape speeds, the distance between peaks becomes smaller [183]. Raising the audio frequency also brings the magnetized sections nearer.

A limit arises when the magnetic 'domain' length from one cycle to the next is smaller than the gap of the head. Then results soon fall off. To help avoid this, head gaps are very small – as small as 0·00025 in.

For music, or when a response up to 10,000cps or so will be wanted, the tape may move at 15 ips, while $7\frac{1}{2}$ ips and $3\frac{3}{4}$ in. per second speeds suit less exacting needs, and $1\frac{7}{8}$ in. per second or slower movement allows satisfactory recording of speech, and gives long playing time with small spools. Two or more tracks also give longer time.

The tape is drawn by a 'capstan', a revolving roller. It may have a heavy flywheel and belt drive [184].

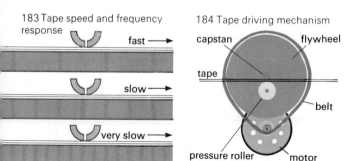

183 Tape speed and frequency response

184 Tape driving mechanism

Playback

To hear the recording, the tape is wound on its original spool, then drawn past a playback head at the same speed as when recorded [185]. The magnetized tape causes a small magnetic field in the head core, thus generating an electrical output. When recording, audio currents produce a varying magnetic field; during playback, the varying of the magnetic field causes audio currents.

In many spheres, of course, such as broadcasting activities, newsgathering, etc., signals may be recorded from sources other than a microphone, e.g. from other tape recordings, from discs or from radio programmes. Signals can also be recorded from television so that playback supplies a picture. Equipment for this is complicated.

For mains use, recorders can employ about four stages, resistance capacity coupled [186]. For better volume and fidelity, push-pull output may be provided.

Record/Playback

The same head may be used to record on the tape, and obtain signals when playing the recording. Switching of

185 Playback of the recording

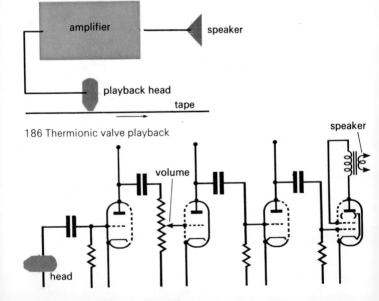

186 Thermionic valve playback

input and output circuits allows the same amplifier to be employed for both purposes [187]. With the switch at **R** (Record) the microphone provides the amplifier input.

For playback (P) the head is switched to the amplifier input, and the output to a loudspeaker. There are two 'outputs', because that for the head is taken from an earlier stage – the full power of a large amplifier is not wanted while recording.

Recording Level Indicator

An indicator shows us that recording is at a suitable level. In Figure 188, X goes to an audio amplifier. The diode rectifies audio signals, building up a negative voltage. This reduces anode current, so the deflector plates become more positive. Electrons from the cathode strike a target, and the beam width is controlled by the deflector plate potential. Hence the display depends on the average audio power, and we adjust volume for correct recording.

If we apply a high frequency 'bias' oscillation to the head while recording, results are improved. The power output stage can be utilized as a bias oscillator. In Figure

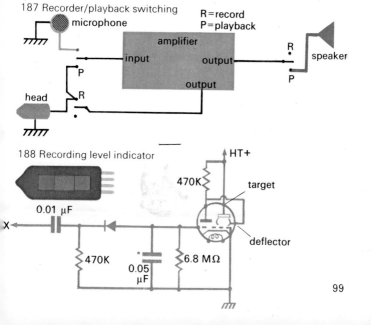

187 Recorder/playback switching

R=record
P=playback

microphone
amplifier
input
output
output
speaker
head

188 Recording level indicator

HT+
470K
target
0.01 µF
X
deflector
470K
6.8 MΩ
0.05 µF

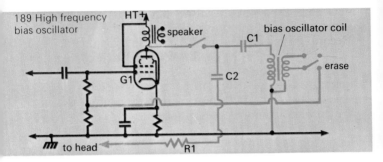

189 High frequency bias oscillator

HT+
speaker
C1
bias oscillator coil
erase
G1
C2
to head
R1

189, C1 couples the oscillator coil, and feedback to G1 sustains oscillation. HF bias is taken through C2 and R1 to the recording head.

To erase a recording, the particles are restored to random orientation. Permanent magnet systems can remove a recording, but a high frequency erase signal is better. The bias oscillator provides a stronger signal, output being from the whole secondary [190]. The tape is drawn past the erasing head, and the rapidly alternating field shifts the magnetic particles into random positions.

The playback head output is not uniform over a wide frequency range, but peaks around 2,500 cycles [191]. Fixed or variable tone control or correction circuits help compensate for this. In figure 191, C1 has low reactance

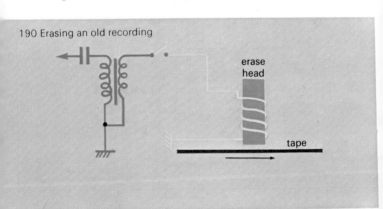

190 Erasing an old recording

erase head

tape

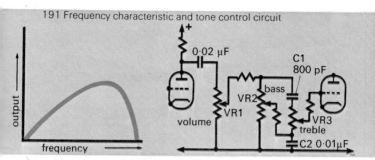

191 Frequency characteristic and tone control circuit

at high frequency, while C2 bypasses high frequencies; thus manipulation of VR3 allows treble to be adjusted.

Transistor Equipment

Figure 192 is a 'pocket' recorder. During recording (R) the microphone supplies signals through C1. Amplified signals reach the head through R1. During playback (P) the head supplies signals through C1, output being to a small speaker. VR1 is for volume control.

There is no HF or erase bias. Erasure is obtained by a permanent magnet, which swamps out the selective orientation of particles during recording. A low-consumption 6 volt motor provides power to drive the capstan. C2 suppresses motor noise.

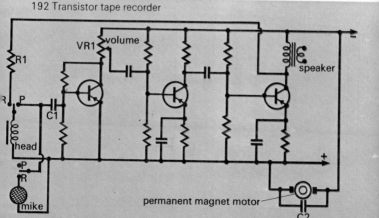

192 Transistor tape recorder

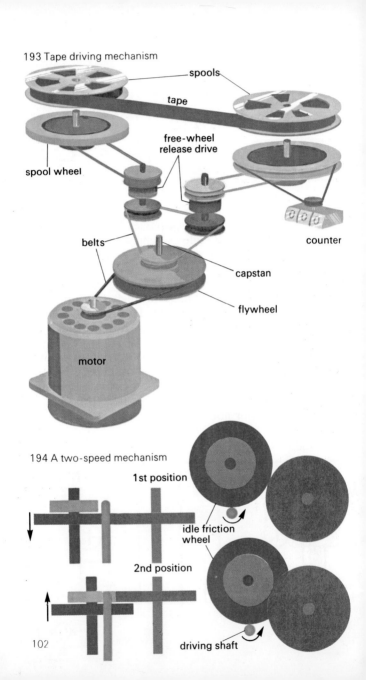

193 Tape driving mechanism

spools

tape

free-wheel
release drive

spool wheel

counter

belts

capstan

flywheel

motor

194 A two-speed mechanism

1st position

idle friction
wheel

2nd position

driving shaft

Drive Mechanism

Figure 193 is a drive mechanism. (Other methods are used.) Here, one motor performs all functions. During recording or playback, a pressure roller keeps the tape in contact with the capstan, and winds it at uniform speed past the head. At the same time, the wheel on which the take-up spool rests turns at the correct speed to take up tape.

To move the tape the other way (for multi-track recording), the motor is reversed, and a free-wheel mechanism transfers the drive to the other spool wheel. For fast rewinding on the original spool, the pressure roller is withdrawn, and the take-up spool revolves at full speed. A belt from one spool wheel drives a mechanical counter, which enables starting positions of items to be noted.

Figure 194 is a speed-change mechanism, allowing a higher speed to be used for music or high fidelity, and a lower speed for speech or longer playing time.

A series of push-buttons often control working, and may operate 2-pole change-over switching contacts [195]. Any button depressed is held by a spring latch common to all buttons. Such switching can change heads, for upper or lower tracks on a tape, and reverse the motor, etc. Many electro-mechanical devices are often incorporated. One is a solenoid which pulls a roller, to press tape against the rotating capstan [196]. When no current flows through the solenoid, the tape is free for rapid winding.

195 Push-button control and heads for two tracks

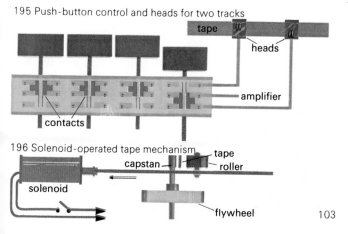

196 Solenoid-operated tape mechanism

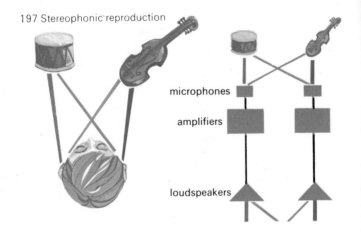

197 Stereophonic reproduction

microphones

amplifiers

loudspeakers

Stereo Reproduction

Stereophonic sound appears to have direction and depth, as we can realize when we hear a live orchestral performance. The effect depends on changes in strength and phase of sounds from different directions [197].

The same effect can be obtained by using two microphones, amplifiers and loudspeakers. A person between the loudspeakers near the third corner of a triangle, the loudspeakers occupying the other corners, seems to hear a live performance.

Stereo disc records have two channels, for right and left, cut in one groove and obtained from right- and left-hand microphones, or directional microphones.

The stereo pick-up stylus can vibrate in two directions. Vibration one way changes the magnetic field in a coil for

198 Stereo from discs

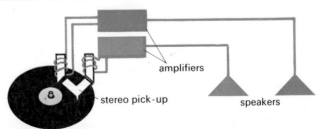

amplifiers

stereo pick-up

speakers

the right-hand output. The other direction produces the left-hand output. Each output goes to its own amplifier and loudspeaker [198].

For stereo tape two or four tracks supply separate left- and right-hand channels [199]. Recording is from two sources and amplifiers. Playback is simultaneously from both tracks, with individual amplifiers and speakers.

For best results, stereo equipment may have high fidelity amplifiers – circuits able to give equal tonal results with little distortion over a wide frequency range.

Video Tape Recording

Frequencies to be retained when recording a TV picture are very much higher than those encountered with sound. With the normal type of tape recorder, the tape speed would have to be impracticably high.

A method of overcoming this is to employ heads equally displaced on the perimeter of a rotating wheel. As a tape $\frac{3}{4}$ in., 1 in., or 2 in. wide passes across the heads the recorded video tracks lie at an angle [200].

Tape speeds depend on the purpose, but may be 15 in. per second or $7\frac{1}{2}$ in. per second, and the latter used with rotating heads gives an effective speed of 75 ft. per second.

199 Twin tracks on tape for stereo

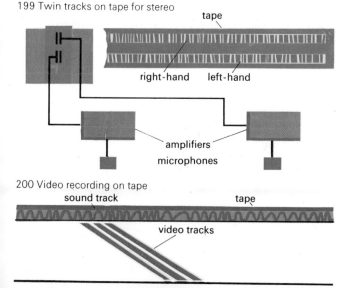

200 Video recording on tape

OTHER APPLICATIONS OF ELECTRONICS

Counting Electronically

Counting circuits record the number of objects produced by a machine, the number of oscillations each second, or speed, or distance. They also show the results of addition, and other operations.

Mechanical Counter

A vehicle mechanical counter shows miles covered. An electricity meter counter shows units consumed. Seeing what actually happens mechanically is useful.

Revolving mechanical counters are often used [201]. Shaft A rotates to display numbers up to 9. When it has rotated from zero to the 10th unit, tooth X rotates the wheel on shaft B one place, moving the tens counter from 0 to 1. This happens with each revolution of A. One complete turn of B rotates the hundreds counter one place, and 99 revolutions of shaft A, counting up to 999, can be accommodated.

A solenoid, pawl and toothed wheel could rotate shaft A. An electrical circuit closes, current flows, and the pawl moves the counter one place. Such devices are occasionally connected after high-speed electronic counters, to record very large numbers.

What actually happens? As shown in Figure 202, each time the full 'units' capacity is reached, one impulse is transferred to the 'tens' counter and the units return to

201 Mechanical counter

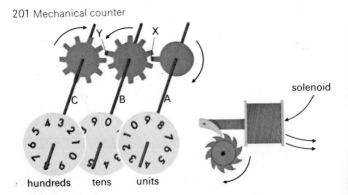

hundreds   tens   units

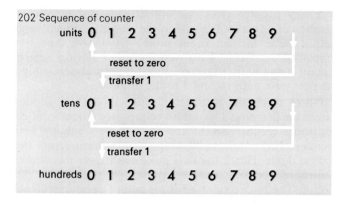

202 Sequence of counter

units 0 1 2 3 4 5 6 7 8 9

reset to zero
transfer 1

tens 0 1 2 3 4 5 6 7 8 9

reset to zero
transfer 1

hundreds 0 1 2 3 4 5 6 7 8 9

zero. Similarly, the full capacity of tens results in one impulse being transferred to the 'hundreds' position.

Electronic circuits giving one output pulse for a number of input pulses similarly form a section of a counter.

Mechanical processes that are repeated can be counted by a closing circuit [203]. The counter is electrically operated. Current from the supply reaches the solenoid each time the circuit closes, moving the units counter. The switch may be operated by weight, or by any means.

Electronic methods perform the same function more reliably, easily and rapidly. Figure 204 has an infra-red light beam falling on a photocell. This causes an electrical output which is amplified. When the beam is interrupted an impulse is passed to the units counter. Every tenth impulse is transferred to the tens counter, and so on.

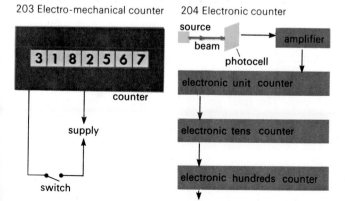

203 Electro-mechanical counter

3 1 8 2 5 6 7

counter

supply

switch

204 Electronic counter

source
beam
photocell
amplifier

electronic unit counter

electronic tens counter

electronic hundreds counter

A ring counter gives one output pulse for a selected number of input pulses – for the decimal system, one output pulse for ten input pulses [205]. We may use controlled rectifiers, thyratrons or other devices which remain stable until 'triggered' by an input pulse, retaining the new state until returned to the original.

Pulses reach the rectifiers through diodes D. Diodes except the first have a large bias voltage from the associated controlled rectifier. So the first pulse triggers only the first rectifier. This conducts, causing a low voltage across the second diode. Hence the next pulse can trigger the second controlled rectifier, and ten pulses progress along the circuit. The last rectifier gives an output pulse to a 'tens' panel, and back to the input to restore the units circuit to zero. Six panels would count up to 999,999.

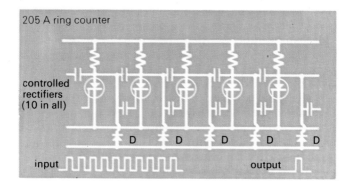

205 A ring counter

controlled rectifiers (10 in all)

input

output

Trochotron and Dekatron

The trochotron has a central cathode, ten grids, ten targets or anodes, and ten electrodes [206]. Grids 1, 3, 5, 7 and 9 are connected to one circuit, and 2, 4, 6, 8 and 0 to another circuit. Suppose the electron stream is at 0. An input pulse cuts off the stream, while grid 1 causes the beam to form on target 1. Each subsequent pulse moves the beam round one step. The final position can transfer one pulse to a 'tens' counting valve. The trochotron can count 1,000,000 a *second*.

The dekatron has ten cathodes. Ionization causes the

discharge path to glow [207]. The X pins are joined and fed from pulses to be counted. Pulses reach the Y pins through a delay circuit. When a pulse arises, pin X near 7 deflects the discharge clockwise, and further deflection arises as the delayed pulse reaches adjacent pin Y. When the pulse ceases, the discharge has been stepped to 8. This can be repeated as many times as required.

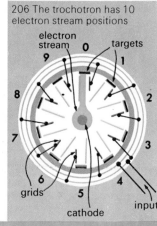

206 The trochotron has 10 electron stream positions

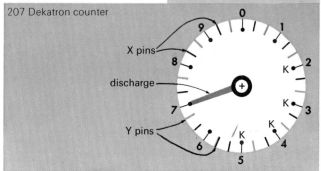

207 Dekatron counter

208 A tube to display numerals

Display Tube

Figure 208 is a tube with electrodes in the shape of the numerals 0 to 9 arranged close together with a common anode. The other ends of the numerals are connected to separate pins. The discharge causes a visible glow round the numeral receiving voltage.

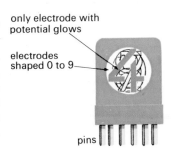

only electrode with potential glows

electrodes shaped 0 to 9

pins

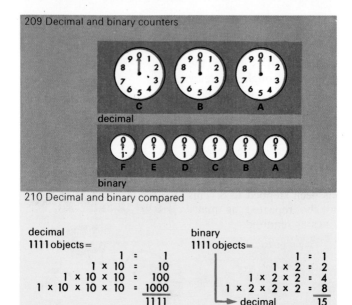

209 Decimal and binary counters

decimal

binary

210 Decimal and binary compared

decimal					binary				
1111 objects =					1111 objects =				

decimal 1111 objects =

	1	=	1
	1 × 10	=	10
1 × 10 × 10		=	100
1 × 10 × 10 × 10		=	1000
			1111

binary 1111 objects =

	1	=	1
	1 × 2	=	2
1 × 2 × 2		=	4
1 × 2 × 2 × 2		=	8
→ decimal			15

The Binary System

We need not count in the form '1, 2, 3, 4, 5, 6, 7, 8, 9, 0 and carry 1'. Electronically there are advantages in counting in other ways. The binary system counts by using 0 and 1. Figure 209 shows two counters, one with 0–9 dials and one for binary. They have rotating pointers. We record objects up to 9 on A of the decimal counter. For 10 we see there is no higher number than 9 here. So we set A to zero and transfer 1 to B. We proceed in this way to 999.

With binary the highest number on any dial is 1. When one object arrives, this is put on A, giving 000001. For object 2 there is no number higher than 1 on A. So we restore A to 0, carrying one to B, to get 000010. For object 3 we put A to 1 again: 000011. The next object results in 0 for A and carry 1, 0 and carry one for B, turning C to 1 = 000100. Similarly, 5 = 000101; 6 = 000110; 7 = 000111; 8 = 001000; 9 = 001001; 10 = 001010, and so on.

Each time we move to the left in decimal counting, we multiply by 10 [210]. Each move to the left in binary multiplies by 2 because there are two possibilities for each column (0 and 1). To register numbers from 0 to 9 in decimal systems, we need *ten* reliable states for an electronic device. For binary, we need *two* – for 0 to 1.

A lack of voltage or current can represent 0, and full voltage or current can show 1. The result is a definite 'on' – 'off' system for each column [211].

Computers

Relays close when energized [212]. Early computers used thousands of relays. Thermionic valve anode current is low with strong negative grid bias, but high with little bias or a positive pulse. The PNP transistor does not conduct with a positive signal at the base, but conducts

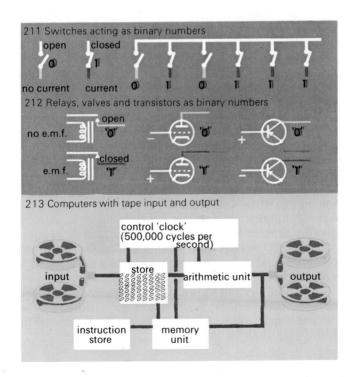

211 Switches acting as binary numbers

open 0   closed 1

no current   current   0 1 0 1 1 1

212 Relays, valves and transistors as binary numbers

no e.m.f.   open '0'   '0'   '0'

e.m.f.   closed '1'   '1'   '1'

213 Computers with tape input and output

control 'clock'
(500,000 cycles per second)

input   store   arithmetic unit   output

instruction store   memory unit

with a negative signal, and working is only 'on' or 'off'. The computer may take input pulses from a tape, store and process them, and deliver the solution or output to a second tape [213].

Bi-Stable or Flip-Flop
Figure 214 shows a circuit that will remain in either of two conditions. If transistor A base is negative, transistor A collector current is large, hence collector C1 is positive, and so is base B2 of transistor B. As a result, collector C2 current is small, and there is little voltage drop across R2, and so base B1 is held negative. An input pulse reverses these conditions. Collector C1 no longer passes a large current and the voltage drop in R1 has fallen, shifting base B2 of transistor B in a negative direction. This transistor conducts, so the increased voltage drop across R2 makes collector C2 positive, and therefore base B1. The circuit thus remains in either state, until a pulse is received. Output can be taken from collector C2.

Any device which can be placed in a steady 'on' or 'off' condition can be used for counting. Binary counters divide by 2 [215]. Decade circuits divide by 10. In counting frequencies, an electronic gate (switch) allows signals to pass for a known interval, while they are counted.

Geiger counters help measure radiation intensity. A central anode of high positive potential is fitted in an envelope of gas mixture [216]. High velocity particles cause ionization. Liberated electrons pass to the positively charged anode, causing small output pulses.

Analog to Digital Conversion
'Analog' information represents a fact in an analogous way. A voltmeter pointer or speedometer pointer position is an analog of voltage or of miles per hour. One means of converting analog to binary digital is shown in Figure 217. A photo-electric eye registers divisions as they pass.

The second method shown has sensing devices opposite the white 0000 sectors. Black sectors are 1. Rotating the disc one step at a time produces the binary count – 0001, 0010, 0011, 0100, etc.

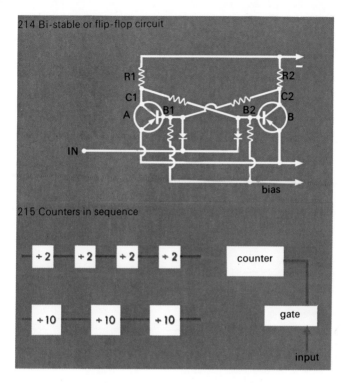

214 Bi-stable or flip-flop circuit

R1 C1 A B1 B2 C2 B R2

IN

bias

215 Counters in sequence

÷2 → ÷2 → ÷2 → ÷2

counter

÷10 → ÷10 → ÷10

gate

input

216 A Geiger counter

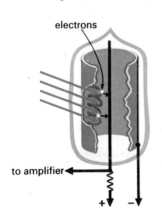

electrons

to amplifier ←

+ −

217 Methods of converting analog to digital

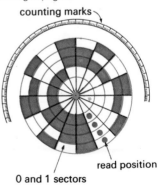

counting marks

read position

0 and 1 sectors

Output-Producing Circuits

Outputs are provided by oscillators, amplifiers, and other circuits, as needed.

If an inductor L and capacitor C are in parallel [218], and a potential momentarily arises in the inductance, the inductor electromagnetic field stores energy. The field collapses, producing an e.m.f. to charge the capacitor. The capacitor discharges, returning power to the inductor. Resistance and other losses cause the oscillations to get smaller and finally cease.

The oscillation frequency or 'resonant' frequency in hertz

$$\text{is } \frac{1}{2\pi\sqrt{LC}}$$

where L is henrys and C farads.

218 Oscillation in circuit having inductance and capacity

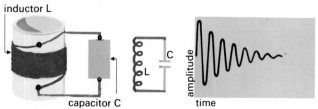

Sustained Oscillation

If we add a device which cancels circuit losses, oscillation continues. Figure 219 has resonant circuit L1 and C. L2 is a coupling winding returning energy to L1. The e.m.f. across L1 reaches the control grid G. An amplified signal arises at anode A, and if L2 feeds back energy to L1 in the correct phase this sustains oscillation.

219 Feedback to sustain oscillation

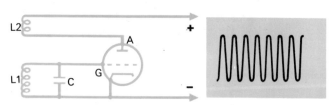

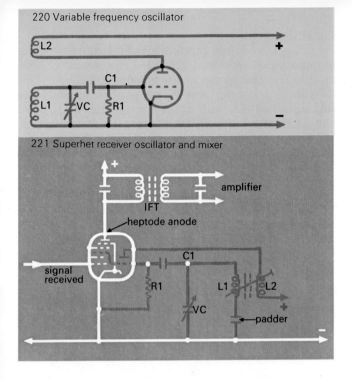

220 Variable frequency oscillator

221 Superhet receiver oscillator and mixer

A variable capacitor VC [220] allows tuning over a band of frequencies. The inductor L1 is changed for other wavebands. Rectification between cathode and grid causes a negative charge to appear across C1 and R1, producing stable working conditions.

A circuit like this is found in most valve radio receivers. The oscillator is the triode part of a triode-hexode, or other 'frequency changer'. Figure 221 has R1, C1, VC, L1 and L2 with the triode section. The triode grid also controls the flow of current to the heptode anode. L1 is tuned so that the difference between the received signal and frequency of L1 is always the same. Mixing in the heptode results in a signal of fixed frequency appearing at the anode. This output passes to the fixed tuned circuits of the intermediate frequency transformer IFT. The 'padder' helps make the coverage of L1 suitable.

Signal Generator

Oscillating circuits can produce a radio frequency output or radio signal. A signal generator is a source of low-power energy that we can tune to any frequency.

Figure 222 has R1 and R2 to provide suitable base working conditions, with emitter resistor R3. L1 is tuned with VC and has a feedback winding L2 to the base B. The output from the arrangement in Figure 222 is a radio frequency signal without modulation. If it is tuned in on an ordinary receiver, no sound is heard. It is termed an 'unmodulated' or 'carrier wave' output. When we need a wave modulated by an audio tone we can add an audio oscillator [223]. This modulates the RF signal. When the signal is tuned in, the audio tone is heard.

A use for the signal generator is in aligning the intermediate frequency transformers of a receiver [224]. Most

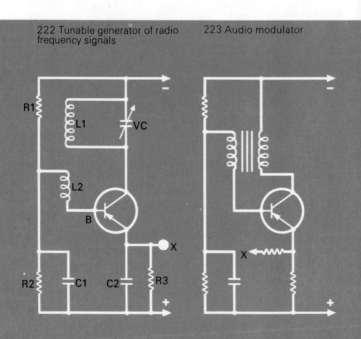

222 Tunable generator of radio frequency signals

223 Audio modulator

IFT's have two tuned circuits, generally with adjustable cores for the coils. Trimmers could be fitted instead. We set the generator tuning to get the required output – often about 470kHz. This is fed into the receiver circuit at a point ahead of the IFT circuits to be adjusted. Then we rotate the cores or trimmers with a trimming tool. Best output from the receiver shows that the circuits are suitably tuned.

The aerial and other tuned circuits in a receiver can be adjusted in this way. We set the generator to suitable frequencies, and adjust trimmers and cores so that wavelengths or frequencies are tuned in at the correct positions on the receiver scale.

Figure 225 is the radio frequency section of a signal generator for the 10–300 megacycle range, and is thus suitable for very high frequency alignment or testing.

224 Use of signal generator to align receiver

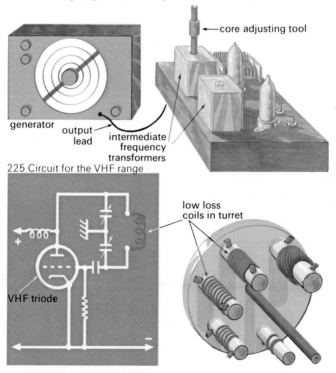

core adjusting tool

generator output lead intermediate frequency transformers

225 Circuit for the VHF range

low loss coils in turret

VHF triode

Multivibrator
The 'multivibrator' circuit produces a wide range of outputs, according to working conditions. It uses two thermionic valves, a double valve, or two transistors [226]. Transistor A has collector resistor R1 and base resistor R2. B has R3 and R4. C1 couples A collector to the base of B, while C2 couples B back to the base of A. With each transistor driving the other, frequency depends largely on capacitor and resistor values. This circuit can produce outputs for receiver or amplifier testing.

Phase-Shift Oscillator
If the voltage of a PNP transistor base is moved positive, collector current falls. Less current flows in the collector resistor, less voltage is dropped here, and the collector potential moves negative. Feedback from collector to base would be in the wrong phase to sustain oscillation – negative when it should be positive, and vice versa. Two transistors, each reversing phase [226], overcome this.

So for a single transistor or thermionic valve we may need some way of reversing phase. Feedback then sustains oscillation. Capacitors and resistors can form a phase-shift circuit for this purpose [227].

Bias Oscillator
Figure 228 obtains oscillation by suitably connecting the primary P and secondary S of the oscillator coil. For example, reversing the connections to S would reverse the phase of feedback to the base. The frequency of oscillation depends on the windings and value of C1. The primary P is tapped for a suitable collector load. Output is taken from another tapping through C2 to provide high frequency bias when tape recording.

Electronic Clock
Figure 229 is a circuit producing low-speed output pulses of great accuracy of occurrence. A piezo-electric crystal oscillator runs at set frequency, and this is stepped down by dividers, to obtain the low-speed output pulses used for timing. The apparatus is controlled by the crystal.

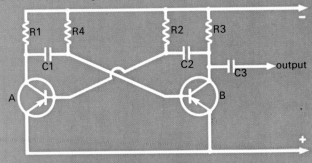

226 Multivibrator using two transistors

R1 R4 R2 R3
C1 C2 C3 → output
A B

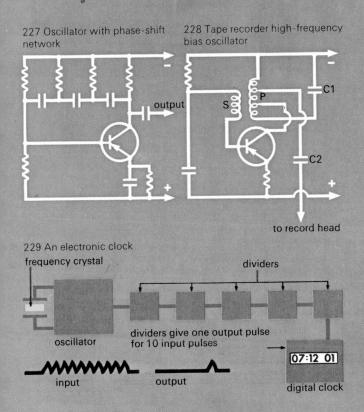

227 Oscillator with phase-shift network

output

228 Tape recorder high-frequency bias oscillator

S P C1
C2
to record head

229 An electronic clock

frequency crystal

dividers

oscillator

dividers give one output pulse
for 10 input pulses

input

output

07:12 01

digital clock

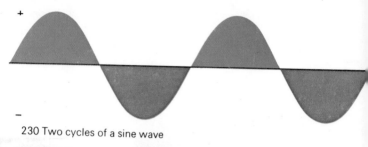

230 Two cycles of a sine wave

231 Two cycles of a square wave

Waveforms

An important wave is the sine wave [230]. This is obtained from alternating current mains. The voltage rises smoothly to a maximum, and falls through zero to a negative value of equal magnitude. If we used an oscilloscope, we would see this happening 50 times each second with 50 cycle per second house supplies. The sine wave could be of other frequency, perhaps a pure audio tone, from a signal generator. 'Frequency' means complete cycles per second.

The smooth rise and fall of voltage and current enables mathematical relations to exist between the peak voltage or current, and the effective voltage or current (which is less). An instrument such as an AC voltmeter cannot respond to the rapid changes, and indicates the effective value. The square wave is useful for test and other purposes. It rises and falls almost instantaneously [231]. It can be produced by generating a sine wave and clipping positive and negative peaks.

The sawtooth wave is quite different [232]. If a capacitor is charged through a series resistor from a high potential

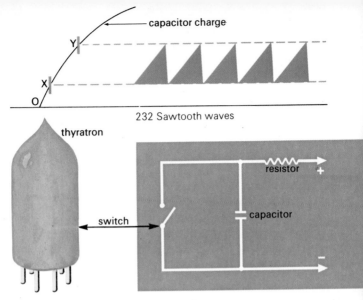

232 Sawtooth waves

233 Circuit for producing sawtooth waves

the voltage across the capacitor rises. One section, from X to Y, is fairly linear ('straight'). To produce sawtooth waves, the capacitor is discharged rapidly when it reaches Y, so the voltage falls to that at X. The capacitor charges again. This is repeated. Rise from X to Y should be without curvature. Descent to X should be almost instant.

Figure 233 shows a circuit for producing sawtooth waves. Current flows through the resistor into the capacitor, so that the charge rises (X to Y). The speed and extent of this rise can be adjusted by selecting capacitor and resistor values and the supply potential. When the charge reaches Y the switch is closed, discharging the capacitor. The switch is then opened, so the charge begins to rise again. In practical circuits, a thyratron can replace the switch. This valve conducts abruptly each time the potential reaches a pre-arranged level (see page 53).

Sawtooth waves are used in an oscilloscope. The slow rise of voltage makes the cathode ray traverse the screen, and the ray returns almost instantaneously when the capacitor is discharged, to begin another sweep.

Radar and Other Devices

Radio waves travel outwards at 300,000,000 metres or 186,000 miles per second.

So if a signal has a frequency of 300,000,000 oscillations a second, the wavelength is 1 metre [234]. The radiated signal has magnetic and electric fields at right angles. Unless reflected by the earth or bent by ionized belts, etc. the signals travel in straight lines.

A directional aerial gives strongest reception of signals when pointed at the transmitter. The direction-finding receiver Rx [235a] takes bearings on transmitters Tx. These bearings on a chart cross to show the receiver position.

If the position of a transmitter Tx is not known [235b] bearings are taken from two positions. The lines cross at the transmitter.

Radio Astronomy

Observations made directly by ordinary telescope are confined to visual frequencies. Photographic time exposures record dim stars. Visible light and similar rays

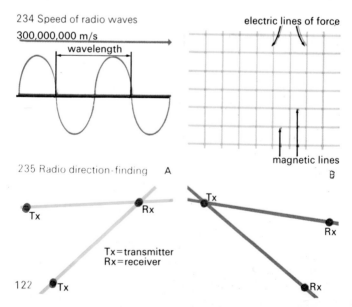

234 Speed of radio waves

300,000,000 m/s

wavelength

electric lines of force

magnetic lines

235 Radio direction-finding A

Tx=transmitter
Rx=receiver

Tx

Rx

Tx

Tx

Rx

Tx

Rx

B

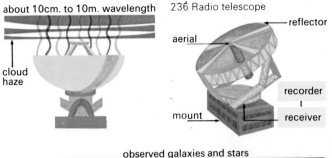

about 10cm. to 10m. wavelength

cloud haze

236 Radio telescope

reflector

aerial

recorder

mount

receiver

observed galaxies and stars

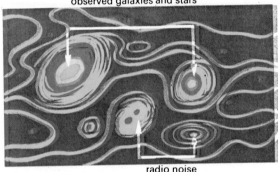

radio noise

237 Visual observation and results of radio astronomy

are absorbed by haze, but radio frequency radiations are of longer wavelength, and are not hindered.

Remote galaxies and systems generate radio 'noise' – that is, random bursts of radio-frequency radiation. A directive aerial can locate the bearing of these. The dish reflector [236] may be hundreds of feet in diameter, and concentrates signals on an aerial. The dish can be pivoted. Signals pass to a sensitive receiver, and are recorded. Radio noise sources are often located near systems observed optically [237]. Sources of radio noise have been mapped at enormous distances, beyond the reach of an optical telescope and where no systems can be seen or photographed. In this way, information has been gathered outside the range of optical observation. Radio waves travel 186,000 miles per second. Radio telescopes have located galaxies over 4,500 million light-years away.

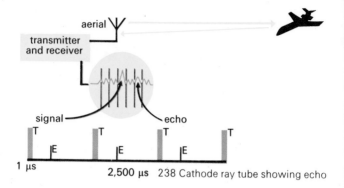

signal

echo

1 μs   2,500 μs   238 Cathode ray tube showing echo

Radio Detection And Ranging (Radar)

If aircraft, etc. are in the path of a radio signal, some energy is reflected as an 'echo' back to the transmitter. In Figure 238 a transmitter radiates 1 micro-second pulses T of very high frequency at 2,500μs intervals and followed by periods in which a receiver picks up echoes E. As signals travel at known speed, the distance of an object is measured by noting the time taken for the echo to return. The interval can be shown by a cathode ray travelling rapidly from left to right across the screen [238]. A scale can be marked in distances.

Plan position radar equipment shows the distance of an object. By rotating a directional aerial [239], and causing the trace to scan from the centre of the tube outwards and rotate with the aerial, the compass bearing of an object is shown, as well as its distance. As the aerial and trace revolve, echoes from surrounding features build up a plan or picture on the screen. The cathode ray may be

239 Rotating aerial and trace for bearing

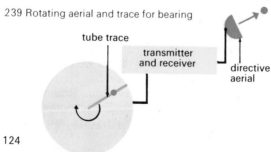

tube trace

transmitter and receiver

directive aerial

brightened at regular intervals to produce range rings [240]. These can be expanded or contracted at the same time as the trace speed is adjusted, to change the 'scale' so that large or small areas can be examined.

Angle marks can also be provided [240].

Some precision-approach radar for ground aid to landing aircraft has two aerial systems. One directive system sweeps a narrow beam in a horizontal plane, and the other sweeps a vertical plane [241]. The two sweeps combine to give a 3-dimensional position for an aircraft – one set of equipment produces the 2-dimensional 'map', the other the height reading, or other dimension.

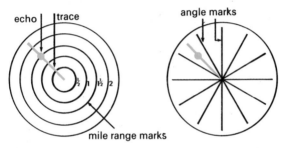

240 Range and angle marks on a plan position radar

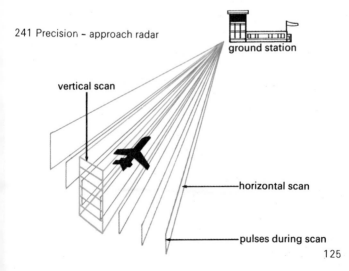

241 Precision – approach radar

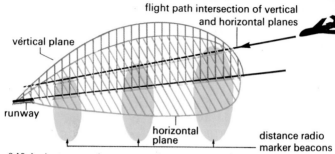

242 An instrument low-approach system

One instrument low-approach system for landing aircraft
has a vertical signal to mark the runway, and a horizontal
signal for the landing path. Beacons radiate vertically at
'outer', 'middle' and 'boundary' positions [242].

Sonar (Sound Navigation And Ranging) systems allow
the distance to be found to the seabed, to a submerged
vessel, etc. High-frequency signals are amplified and passed
to an electronic switch circuit, which directs them to a
transducer [243]. Echoes are diverted to a receiver by the
electronic switch, and the delay allows the cathode ray
tube to give a distance reading.

Pictures by Radio

News pictures, etc. can be sent across the world by radio.
A picture secured to a rotating drum can be scanned
electronically in lines which lie closely side by side [244].
Radio signals corresponding to light and dark areas are
produced. At the receiver, a drum rotates at the same
speed, and a writing head slowly moves the length of the

243 Sonar sound-navigation and ranging

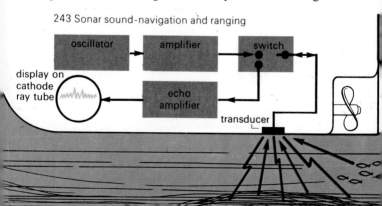

drum, producing light and dark marks. So a complete picture is built up during many rotations of the drum.

Radio signals for pictures may be tape-recorded for storage, or for re-transmission when long-distance short-wave radio conditions are suitable. To synchronize a tape, the tape can have two tracks, one for picture information, and the other recording from a crystal oscillator. These signals are amplified and applied to a phonic motor, the speed of which depends on the frequency [245]. A second motor receives amplified signals from a second crystal oscillator, and rotation operates a differential gear. If the motor running from the taped signals changes speed, the differential gear cage turns. This operates a correction circuit which increases or reduces the tape motor speed. So movement of the tape is synchronized.

244 Pictures by radio

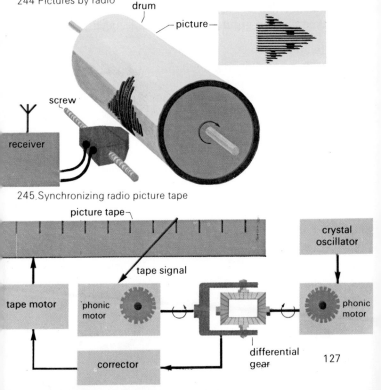

245 Synchronizing radio picture tape

127

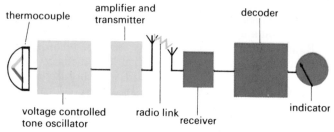

246 Radio telemetry for temperature information

Telemetry is conveying information from instruments to a recording device at a distance – for example, from a satellite to earth. One way is to convert the 'information' into an audio tone, which changes to convey data. As an example, a thermocouple produces a voltage which changes with temperature. This can be taken to an oscillator whose frequency changes with voltage. The tone is transmitted, picked up by a ground station, and decoded [246].

Satellites

Satellites can investigate conditions far above the earth, and send radio reports to ground stations. One employs an orthicon camera to take cloud pictures [247]. Pictures may be taken in daylight and are stored on tape in the satellite. When it is within range of a receiving station, the taped signals are radiated for decoding and printing.

A satellite can measure electron temperature, galactic radio noise, earth generated noise, oxygen density and

247 Weather satellite

camera 'photographs' continental cloud cover

satellite radios pictures to ground station

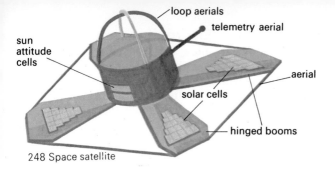

248 Space satellite

other factors. In Figure 248 winged booms with solar cells produce current to operate internal equipment, and to charge storage batteries. Loop, extended and other aerials transmit and receive signals, to convey information to earth, or receive commands. Channels for radio signals are in the high frequency bands. Sun attitude cells receive illumination according to their bearing with relation to the sun's rays, and this can convey information on the tilt or rotation of the satellite.

A relay satellite can be situated thousands of miles above the earth, in a stationary orbit. Solar cells generate power. The satellite has aerials and equipment to receive transmissions, and re-transmit them on a changed frequency [249]. Transmissions are received on the ground by a large paraboloid aerial, which reflects signals to a focus at a pick-up point. The efficiency of such aerials is many thousands of times greater than that of an ordinary aerial and the receiver is specially designed for high sensitivity.

249 Radio relay by space satellite

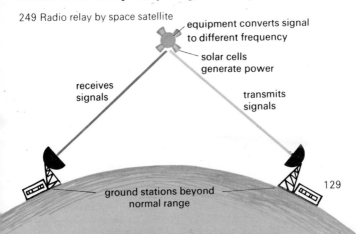

Measurements in Electronic Circuits

Various measurements allow the working conditions of a circuit to be found. The simplest measurements are those which show a steady or uniform voltage or current.

A moving-coil meter winding is in a strong magnetic field, and receives current through hairsprings [250]. It turns slightly when current flows. This meter has a 'full scale deflection' or FSD of 6mA. A current of 6 milliamperes would move the pointer fully across the scale.

Current Through a Resistance = Voltage Divided by Resistance. So resistors in series with the meter allow voltages to be read.

Figure 251 has R1, R2 and R3 for ranges of 2·5 volts, 10 volts and 100 volts, and a 0·25mA meter. So R1 is 10,000 ohms; R2, 40,000 ohms; R3, 400,000 ohms.

To measure heavier currents we connect a resistor across the meter. Suppose $\frac{9}{10}$ of the total current flows through this resistor, and only $\frac{1}{10}$ through the meter [252]. The original range is multiplied 10 times.

The multi-range instrument in Figure 253 has a switch with nine positions.

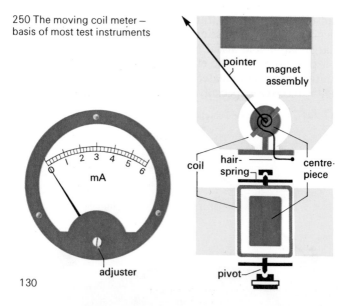

250 The moving coil meter — basis of most test instruments

mA

pointer

magnet assembly

coil

hair-spring

centre-piece

adjuster

pivot

At 1, R1 is in circuit for a voltage range. Positions 2, 3 and 4 give other voltage ranges. R2, R3 and R4 are in series, so that the higher voltages are not across a single resistor. Positions 6, 7, 8 and 9 move along a tapped shunt for higher current ranges. The shunt is permanently across the meter. Suppose the meter has a FSD of 0·5mA, or 1mA FSD with the shunt added. Then R1 is 2·5k for 2·5 volts, R2 is 10k for 10 volts, R3 is 90k for 100 volts (10k already present) and R4 is 150k for 250 volts (10k plus 90k already in the circuit).

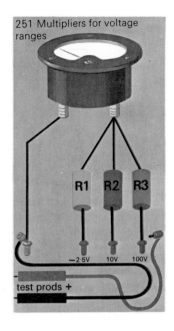

251 Multipliers for voltage ranges

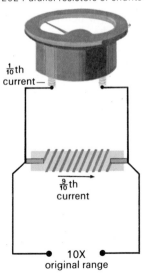

252 Parallel resistors or shunts

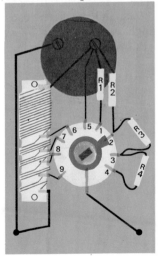

253 A multi-range meter circuit

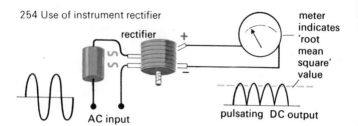

254 Use of instrument rectifier

meter indicates 'root mean square' value

rectifier

AC input

pulsating DC output

Alternating Current

The moving coil cannot respond to AC. For AC ranges we add a rectifier [254] to a meter like that in Figure 250. This changes AC to pulsating DC. The meter shows the 'Root mean square' or effective value – what we generally need to know. 'Effective' value is that which has the same heating effect or 'power' as equivalent direct current.

Resistances Too

We may need to measure resistance values. We use a battery, variable resistor VR, fixed resistor R, and the meter all in series [255]. We join test leads from the sockets together and adjust VR until the meter reads full scale. This is *zero ohms*. If we separate the test leads, no current flows, and the meter reads zero current, which is infinitely high resistance, or *infinity*. If we take the leads to a resistor, or circuit being tested, the meter will indicate

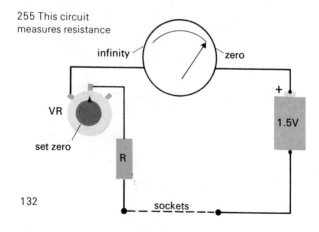

255 This circuit measures resistance

infinity

zero

VR

set zero

R

1.5V

sockets

some intermediate current, depending on the resistance in the circuit. From Ohm's Law we can make a scale for the meter, showing resistance values.

A 'bridge' [256] permits accurate determination of resistance.

If $\dfrac{Ra}{Rb} = \dfrac{Rx}{Rc}$ there is no e.m.f. across the detector.

Rx is the resistance to be measured and Rc an accurately calibrated variable resistor, or a decade box with values selected by switches. Ra and Rb are of known value or ratio. We find the value of Rx by noting what value of Rc produces no current at the detector.

256 Bridge measuring circuit

$$RX = \frac{RA}{RB}\, RC$$

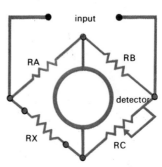

Power Also

Power in Watts $= I^2R$ that is, *Current Squared × Resistance*. A known resistance in series with a meter allows watts to be found [257]. This is handy for some uses. Suppose R is 50 ohms and I is 2 amperes: $2 \times 2 \times 50 = 200$ watts.

Sometimes voltage drop across a resistance may be more readily found. Suppose R is a 2 ohm resistor replacing a loudspeaker and V proves to be 3 volts. From $watts = \dfrac{V^2}{R} = \dfrac{3 \times 3}{2} = \dfrac{9}{2}$ we find that our amplifier is delivering 4·5 watts of audio power.

For direct current circuits, a DC meter is used. But for radio frequency, audio frequency, or alternating current circuits we must use a meter of appropriate type. Popular multi-range meters have scales, with range, AC/DC and ohms controls [258]. The switches bring into use the various parts of the circuit wanted.

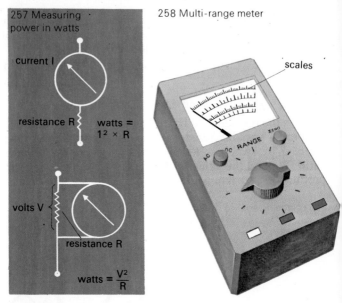

257 Measuring power in watts

current I

resistance R

$$\text{watts} = I^2 \times R$$

volts V

resistance R

$$\text{watts} = \frac{V^2}{R}$$

258 Multi-range meter

scales

Millivoltmeters

A thermionic valve anode current changes with grid voltage. An anode meter can be calibrated in terms of voltage at the grid. Voltages to be tested are placed across a high value resistor R1 [259]. A range switch with resistors R1, R2, R3, etc. could be added.

An electrometer valve allows extremely small voltages to be measured. The valve is very sensitive to grid voltage,

259 Vacuum valve voltmeter

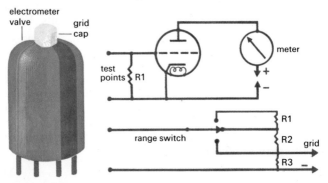

electrometer valve

grid cap

meter

test points

R1

+

−

range switch

R1

R2

R3

grid

−

and so it has a cap for this connection, to avoid leakage.

Electrometer circuits are used to investigate exceedingly low voltages and currents, and to test circuits where current is too small for a moving-coil meter.

Sensitivity can be raised by using an amplifier [260]. V1 is the electrometer valve. Changes in anode current produce a change in voltage across R2. This is taken through R3 to V2, so changing anode current through R4. With no input, VR1 is adjusted until the current through R5 is equal to that through R4, when the meter gives no

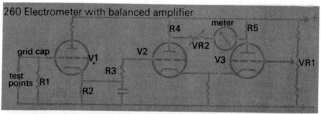

260 Electrometer with balanced amplifier

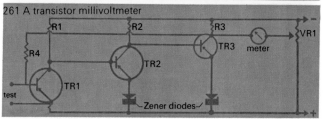

261 A transistor millivoltmeter

reading. Low current or voltage at the 'Test Points' produces a reading on the meter. VR2 adjusts sensitivity.

The amplification from transistors allows sensitive measuring instruments to be made [261]. Here, a low voltage or current at 'Test' changes TR1 current, which flows through R1. This changes TR2 current through R2, which in turn changes TR3 current through R3. VR1 is first set for no reading, with no input. Zener diodes stabilize the emitter voltages of TR2 and TR3 because they maintain a certain voltage. The three transistors each amplify in series. Balanced circuits are often used to avoid errors due to transistors drifting.

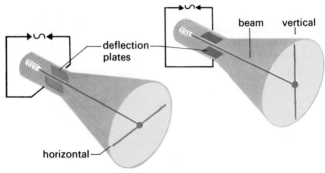

262 Use of oscilloscope for testing

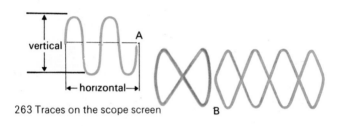

263 Traces on the scope screen

Oscilloscope

A cathode ray tube will display transitory phenomena, such as changes in current or voltage not shown by a meter. The cathode ray strikes the screen centre, producing a luminous spot [262]. Applying an alternating potential to the vertical plates deflects the beam up and down, making a vertical line. This can show voltage. An alternating potential on the horizontal plates results in a horizontal line. By combining horizontal and vertical deflections we can display various events.

If we let an AC potential cause vertical scan, with horizontal scan from a sawtooth oscillator, we get a picture of the wave [263a]. Or we can take inputs to vertical and horizontal plates, causing wavy patterns in which the number of loops shows the relationship between one frequency and the other [263b].

The signals may need amplification[264]. Signals pass to the 'vertical amplifier' which raises the strength of weak inputs. The 'time base' is the generator of sawtooth waves, which sweep the spot across the screen. The 'sync' or synchronizing circuit takes a small part of the input signal and uses it to trigger the time-base, so that complicated traces remain stationary on the screen. A 'horizontal' amplifier may be brought into use. Then another signal can move the spot horizontally. A 'power supply' provides current for each section, and for the tube, which may require 1,000 volts or more, at low current.

All sorts of phenomena can be displayed by the oscilloscope. For example, if an amplifier introduces third harmonic distortion the addition of this to the fundamental frequency produces an unpleasant result [265].

264 Cathode-ray oscilloscope

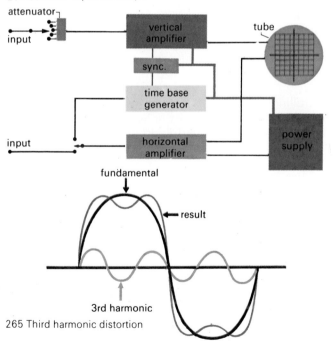

265 Third harmonic distortion

More Uses for Electronics

Electronics does remarkable things – if a process is wanted, an electronic circuit is usually possible.

Petrol Pump

An electronic petrol pump can replace the familiar electrical pump. Coils on the pump are the windings for a low frequency oscillator [266], so the collector and coil current rises and falls. Valves in the plunger and cylinder transform the rapid plunger movement into a steady petrol line pressure, exerted by the spring. This provides a constant supply to the carburettor.

Interval Timer

An interval timer can automatically time a short period, and this can be repeated as often as is needed.

An electronic timer in Figure 267 makes use of the time constant of the large capacitor C. Transistor collector current holds the relay armature down. When the collector current falls, the armature is released. The potentiometer can be calibrated in seconds. Closing and opening of the relay contacts can control other apparatus.

Controlling Currents

The silicon-controlled rectifier or SCR can be turned on by applying current to a control electrode [268]. The SCR can deal with high power for motors and other appliances.

266 Transistorized petrol pump for vehicles   267 Transistorized interval timer

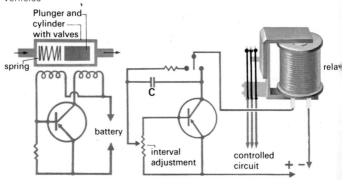

Plunger and cylinder with valves

spring

battery

C

interval adjustment

relay

controlled circuit

+ –

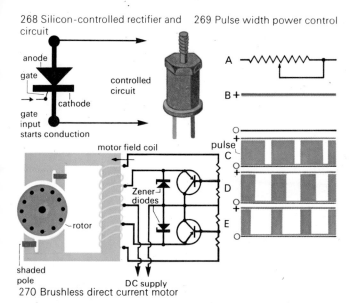

268 Silicon-controlled rectifier and circuit

269 Pulse width power control

anode
gate
controlled circuit
cathode
gate input starts conduction

A
B +

pulse
C
D
E

motor field coil
Zener diodes
rotor
shaded pole

DC supply

270 Brushless direct current motor

A gate-controlled switch or GCS is somewhat similar in effect. The speed of a direct current electric motor can be reduced by a variable resistance in one conductor: voltage to the motor is less [269a]. This wastes unused power as heat in the resistance. Another way is to employ a 'pulse width' oscillator to control a solid state rectifier which allows current to reach the motor. At [269b] current is present the whole time for full speed. In Figure 269c short 'off' intervals reduce the average motor current. In Figures 269d and 269e the 'off' intervals are longer, reducing speed further. No power is wasted in heat.

Brushless DC Motor

The brushes of a DC motor can be noisy; they wear out, and the sparking may be dangerous. The brushless direct current motor employs power transistors to cause an oscillating current [270]. The motor has shaded pole windings, as used for an AC machine, and needs no brushes or commutator.

139

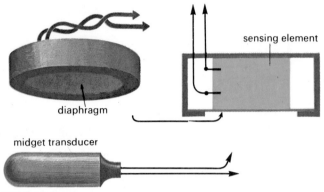

271 Transducers

Transducers and Ultrasonics

A 'transducer' supplies an electrical signal under the influence of pressure or other effects. A pressure transducer [271] alters its electrical resistance with changes in pressure, and so can operate a meter or other indicator. Microminiature pressure transducers have elements formed in silicon crystal, and may be fitted to engine parts, or even in the human body.

In ultrasonic flaw detection [272], steel bars or other materials tested receive the ultrasonic waves upon one surface. The bars may move through a tank, or the equipment may rest on the objects tested. The ultrasonic wave

272 Ultrasonic flaw detection

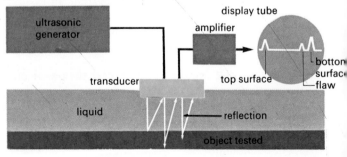

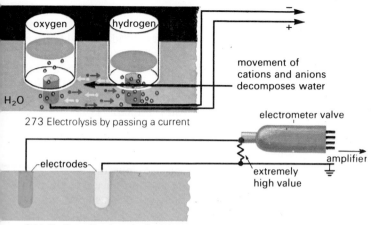

273 Electrolysis by passing a current

274 Finding pH value of a liquid

is reflected by the more distant surface, and by internal flaws. A cathode ray tube shows the interval taken for the reflection, and thus whether a flaw is present.

Another use for ultrasonic equipment is in transmitting signals from a vessel into the water and receiving echoes from the sea bed, fish shoals, etc. The time for the echo to return depends on the distance. (See also page 126.)

Electro-Analysis

Various methods allow chemical analysis by electronic means. In electrolysis, compounds are chemically separated by the passage of an electric current. In the electrolysis of water, hydrogen arises at the negative electrode, and oxygen at the positive electrode [273]. Ions migrating in the direction of the positive current are called cations, while those moving in the direction of the negative current are anions. Substances in solution may be deposited upon neutral electrodes, and afterwards weighed.

The degree of acidity or pH value can be found by a sensitive instrument with immersed electrodes. One electrode is neutral and the other responds to the pH value, so the output from the electrodes depends on this. An extremely sensitive measuring circuit is needed [274].

More Semiconductor Effects

Gallium phosphide alloyed junction diodes and gallium arsenide diffused junction diodes produce light when current is passed in the forward or conducting direction. The gallium arsenide diode junction region has a high concentration of electrons and positive carriers. Photons are emitted when electrons change their energy level. The diode is a form of semiconductor laser or light amplifier – photons travelling along the junction region stimulate re-combination and extra photon emission, so producing more light [275].

Stimulation of a junction by light photons produces a current. A small-current diode may produce one electron for each photon [276]. In the avalanche silicon photo-diode, a potential is applied across the junction. The photons have a higher energy level, and more electrons are liberated. In the photo-transistor, the photo-diode junction forms the base-emitter elements, and transistor action amplifies the base current, so a larger collector current flows from a battery [276].

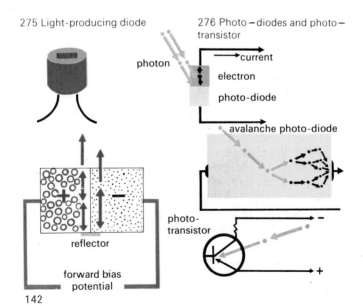

275 Light-producing diode

276 Photo–diodes and photo–transistor

photon

current

electron

photo-diode

avalanche photo-diode

reflector

forward bias potential

photo-transistor

The Field-Effect Transistor

This has source, gate and drain connections. It is P-channel or N-channel. Figure 277 is a field-effect transistor with a P-type gate in the N-type channel. Electron carriers flow from the source to the drain. Changing the gate voltage alters the current which can flow through channel and external circuit. With no gate potential, the channel is at maximum width, A. Current passes readily. With a small negative voltage at the gate, the channel is depleted of carriers, and therefore is smaller, B. This reduces current. Increasing the voltage causes the channel to become narrower until it is 'pinched off' or scarcely able to conduct at all, C. The transistor has a high input resistance. It imposes a smaller load on a circuit that supplies the gate. Ordinary transistors are operated by the current flow at the base, and thus draw a current which loads the base circuit. The field-effect transistor is controlled by the voltage. Figure 278 is a field-effect transistor audio amplifier. This type of transistor is rapidly becoming more popular in radio and other equipment.

277 A field-effect transistor   278 F.E.T. amplifier circuit

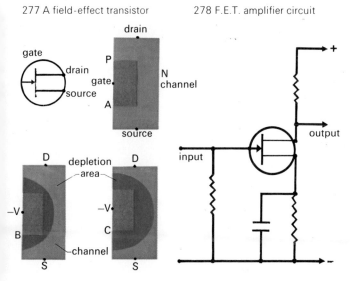

143

Television Cameras

A TV camera supplies a video signal, afterwards amplified and radiated from a transmitter. As the whole scene cannot be changed simultaneously into electrical signals, it is 'scanned' or covered in regular lines. Covering the picture area constitutes a 'frame'. Frames can follow each other with sufficient rapidity to avoid flickering.

A TV picture is built up by a tiny spot of light from the cathode ray, which traverses the screen rapidly. A TV camera performs the reverse action, generating signals which correspond to the light and shade of the scene transmitted. With space vehicles, etc., the impulses may be stored on tape, later used to supply the transmitter.

Figure 279 shows how a picture area is scanned or sampled by a moving area X of small size. During one frame, the small area X has covered the whole picture. (See the section on TV receivers, page 88.)

A camera lens throws an image of the scene on a film [280]. A variable focal-length (zoom) lens, or interchangeable lenses, can give a choice of ordinary, wide-angle, close-up and other views.

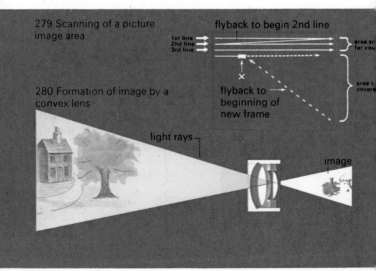

279 Scanning of a picture image area

1st line
2nd line
3rd line

flyback to begin 2nd line

area s… far co…

area t… covere…

×

flyback to beginning of new frame

280 Formation of image by a convex lens

light rays

image

The image orthicon camera optical system projects an image on the photocathode [281]. When light strikes the photocathode, photoelectrons are emitted from the other side. They are most numerous at bright areas of the image. An electric field attracts them to the target. This is extremely thin glass covered by a wire mesh having very many holes per square inch. The photoelectrons knock electrons from the glass, leaving a positive charge. So the positions and intensity of the positive charges correspond to light areas of the image.

The beam from an electron gun scans the back of the glass. When passing over an area where there is a positive charge, the beam leaves electrons to neutralize the charge. When the beam passes over an uncharged area, few if any of the electrons are left. Thus the beam current corresponds to light or dark picture features. An electron multiplier amplifies the changes in beam current. A series of electrodes receive progressively higher voltages [282]. Electrons striking these electrodes cause secondary electrons to be liberated, and the intensified signal can be passed on to other amplifiers.

281 Image orthicon used in TV camera

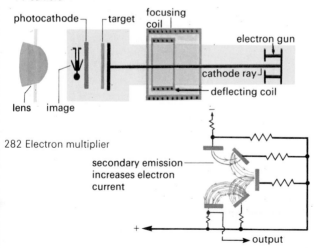

photocathode   target   focusing coil   electron gun

cathode ray

deflecting coil

lens   image

282 Electron multiplier

secondary emission increases electron current

output

Logic Gates

Processes of logic can be carried out by 'gates' whose output depends on the logical process or 'truth' required. Computers use very many of these gates. Figure 283 is a 2-input AND gate. Input pulses arrive at A and B. Transistors 1 and 2 are normally non-conducting. There is no current through R1, no voltage drop here. Transistor 3 base is negative. Current flow through R2 causes a large voltage drop. Output level remains near zero (positive).

A pulse at A or B makes one transistor conduct, but no current flows in R1 unless *both* conduct simultaneously – that is, when pulses arrive at A *and* B together. Then voltage drop in R1 moves collector C positive, transistor 3 ceases to conduct, and a negative pulse appears in the output. Figure 284 is a 2-input OR gate. A pulse at either A OR B will cause an output pulse. Such units may operate at 500,000 pulses or more a second. They work with low voltage (typically 5 volts) and require little power.

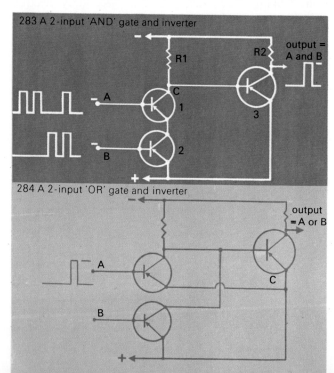

283 A 2-input 'AND' gate and inverter

284 A 2-input 'OR' gate and inverter

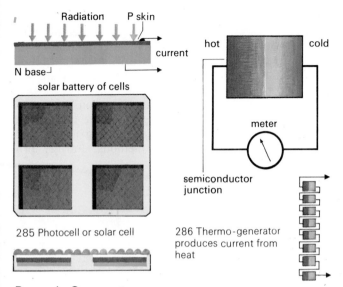

285 Photocell or solar cell

286 Thermo-generator produces current from heat

Power in Space, etc.

Various unconventional ways of generating electrical power have been used in Polar weather stations, for unattended warning lights, satellites, space probes, etc.

A convenient source of power for a space probe is the solar cell. Silicon solar cells have an N-type base containing antimony or other impurity, and a P-type surface layer. Photons or light from the sun striking the cell cause extra electron and hole pairs, and a current which flows through an external circuit [285]. This produces about 0·5 volt. The solar battery can charge accumulator type cells, which provide power for equipment requiring more current, and when the satellite is in darkness.

The thermo-generator is an improvement on the thermocouple. In N-type material, electrons move away from a heat source. So a device can be made in which current is produced if one surface is hot, and the other cold [286]. The heat is a by-product of environment (solar) or of relevant activity. In a reverse or 'refrigeration' system the passage of an electric current makes a semiconductor junction drop in temperature.

Looking Ahead

Analysis of gases, etc., once needing considerable time, can be completed almost instantly. After ionization, the particles are accelerated down a drift tube [287]. Low mass ions accelerate most rapidly, so the ions are separated according to mass.

'Printed circuits' have revolutionized construction of miniature equipment. Conducting paths are arranged to run without overlapping. A large drawing is prepared, and reduced by photocopying methods. Further pro-

287 High-speed spectrometer

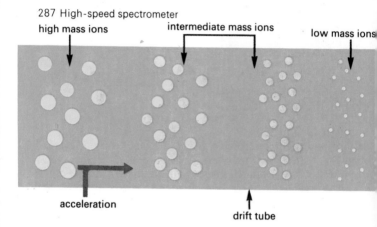

high mass ions   intermediate mass ions   low mass ions

acceleration

drift tube

cessing leaves printed copper conductors [288]. Large numbers of similar panels are readily made. When components are fitted, the printed conductors act as wiring.

Printed circuits and similar methods lead to the production of modules, or small units of similar type. A defective unit is removed as a whole, and replaced by one in working order.

Computers contain thousands of 'logic' elements, such as those for AND and OR functions. These and other circuit units can be tested automatically at high speed by a machine which applies suitable signals, and records the outputs [289]. Errors in outputs from the unit result in it being set aside for repair.

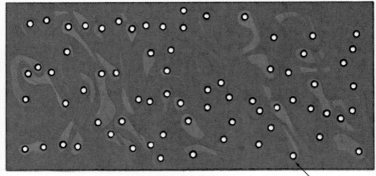

288 Underside of a printed circuit

foil conductors

289 Automated module testing

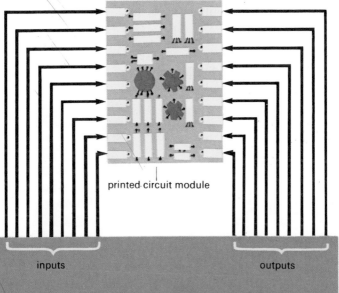

printed circuit module

inputs

outputs

equipment providing
automatic test
programme

A Step Smaller

Even miniature individual resistors have wire ends and occupy unnecessary space. Instead, resistor material can be deposited directly on an insulated panel, between conductors [290]. The resistor has almost no thickness. If the process is carefully controlled, the resistors will be reasonably accurate in value. For high accuracy, the resistor is made a little low in value, and the value is increased by cutting or etching material away.

Conventional capacitors are of foil, separated by insulating paper; or have sheets of mica to separate the plates, or consist of conductive deposits on an insulator. Capacitors of almost no thickness are made [291]. Conducting layer A is deposited, then the insulator or dielectric B. A further conducting layer C is deposited on the insulator. Surfaces A and C form the capacitor.

Thin Films

In microminiature circuits, the insulating base or panel is the 'substrate'. Surface roughness would result in

290 Thin film resistors

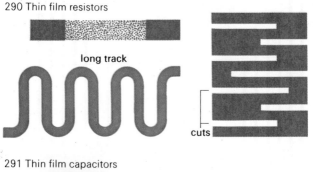

long track

cuts

291 Thin film capacitors

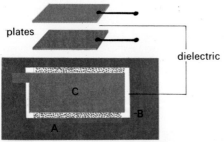

plates

dielectric

C

B

A

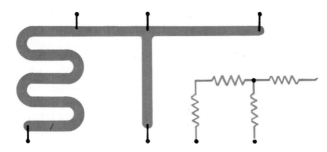

292 Thin film resistor network

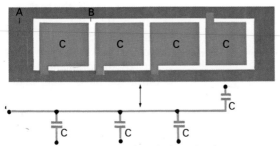

293 Thin film capacitors and equivalent circuit

irregular deposits, so ceramic, glass, and other smooth substrates are used.

Resistors can be deposited nichrome, of extreme thinness, and resistance paths can be shaped as wanted, and tapped if required [292].

One method is to cover a prepared substrate chip with lacquer and photoresist, so that when the pattern is printed and etched the nichrome can afterwards be deposited, giving the required thickness and shape.

Capacitors are made by depositing aluminium, then the dielectric (insulator), then aluminium again. The dielectric may be magnesium fluoride, zinc sulphide, silicon monoxide, or other material. For high capacities in small size, the film is very thin.

Deposits can be shaped to give the desired result. In Figure 293 the single conductor surface A is covered with dielectric B, then four top surfaces C, thus obtaining the equivalent of four capacitors.

151

294 Resistance capacitor network

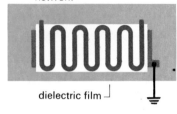

dielectric film

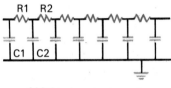

R1   R2

C1   C2

295 Semiconductor and microminiature components

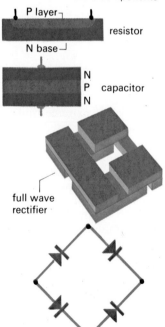

P layer

resistor

N base

N
P   capacitor
N

full wave rectifier

Other Units

Figure 294 has a resistance element, then a dielectric or insulator. A film of conducting material is deposited on the insulator, so there is capacity from it to the resistor throughout its length. This is approximately equivalent to a number of individual resistors R1, R2, etc. with small capacitors C1, C2, etc. Phase shift networks for oscillators and other purposes have been made in this way.

A completed microminiature chip having resistors, capacitors and interconnecting conductors can be of extremely small size. The chip could be 0·1mm. thick, or less, and have many components in an area of a few square millimetres. A number of chips can be placed one on top of another, to build up a thicker whole, or cube, in which are many circuits.

Semiconductors Too

Semiconductor material can be fabricated into microminiature circuit elements. Silicon is preferred, for some increase in temperature is less important than it is with germanium.

A resistor is obtained by having a thin track of P-type material in the N-type base [295]. Capacitors can be derived by having N-type material separated by P-type material. Arrangements of suitably chosen material can provide more complicated circuit equivalents, such as the full-wave bridge rectifier.

Effects present in conventional semiconductor devices can be employed. In Figure 296 the variable capacitor has two metal plates, which are moved to change the capacity. In the semiconductor variable capacity diode, capacity exists between the carrier areas. Applying a bias voltage effectively moves these areas together or apart, so altering the capacity.

Planar transistors occupy little space and thickness. Another method adopted is shown in Figure 297. A base carries a resistance element acting as three resistors in series, with conductor strips A, B and C. Transistors are formed on the material. Input to X or Y will cause a voltage drop in R1, so that a pulse is obtained at B. This is a computer 'OR' gate.

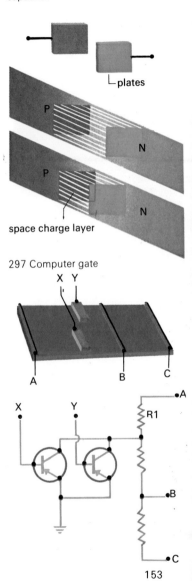

296 Semiconductor variable capacitor

plates

P

N

P

N

space charge layer

297 Computer gate

X Y

A   B   C

X   Y   •A
                R1

                •B

                •C

153

Figure 298 is a microminiature circuit formed by diffusion processes in a piece of semiconductor. With suitable external connections, it may form part of an amplifier, counter, oscillator, etc. With direct couplings and complementary circuits having PNP and NPN transistors, full use can be made of microminiaturization techniques.

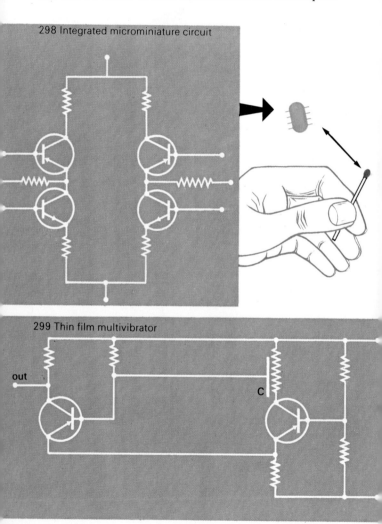

298 Integrated microminiature circuit

299 Thin film multivibrator

out

C

Figure 299 is a thin film multivibrator or oscillator, which requires only the distributed capacity resistor C for feedback, in conjunction with directly connected emitters.

Thin metal film resistors can be cut by electron beam. A powerful discharge tube produces a beam concentrated electromagnetically to a point 0·0005 in. in diameter. The beam is moved by magnetic deflection [300]. The process is carried out by automatic mechanisms [301].

It is interesting to imagine what electronics may accomplish in the future. A tidy picture of a central nucleus surrounded by negative electrons racing round at unimaginable speed does well for many purposes. But much is still unknown. Many discoveries will be made.

300 Thin film resistors cut by electron beam

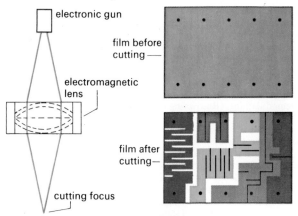

301 Automated production of electronic units

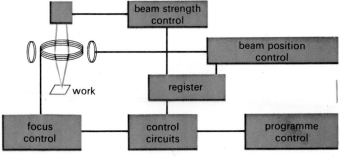

GLOSSARY

Ampere: Unit of current.

Amplitude Modulation: Method of transmitting speech, etc.

Anode: Thermionic valve electrode normally receiving positive supply.

Audio Amplifier: An amplifier which increases the strength of audible signals.

Auto-Transformer: One having tapped winding, instead of separate windings.

Bias: Usually steady voltage applied to obtain suitable working conditions.

Binary: Counting with 0 and 1 only.

Capstan: Rotating part causing steady movement of tape.

Cathode: Thermionic valve electrode emitting electrons; or semiconductor equivalent.

Class A: Amplification of the whole cycle.

Demodulation: Recovering the modulation or sound from a programme.

Dielectric: Insulator (or air) between plates of a capacitor.

Dynamic Working: Actual operational working, as compared with static conditions.

Erasing (Tape): Restoring tape to original non-magnetized state.

Flip-Flop: Circuit which stays in either of two conditions.

Grid: Mesh electrode in thermionic valves.

Grounded: Connected to ground or earth, actually or effectively.

Harmonics: Vibrations or signals at multiples of original.

Heater: Thermionic valve element heated by passage of current.

Heat Sink: Plate, etc. carrying away heat.

Henry: Unit of inductance.

Hertz: Unit of frequency.

Inductor: Coil, etc. possessing inductance.

Logic Gate: Circuit which performs an action of logic.

Module: Small or standard unit.

Multivibrator: Type of oscillator.

Non-Inductive: Resistor, etc. designed to avoid effects of inductance.

Ohm: Unit of resistance.

Optimum Load: Best working load for a transistor, valve, or other device.

Oscilloscope: Instrument which displays waveforms, etc. on cathode ray tube screen.

Phonic Motor: Motor whose speed is related to frequency of supply.

Polarization (Aerial): Vertical or horizontal placement of elements.

Radar: Radio Detection And Ranging.

Rectifier: Device allowing current to pass easily in one direction only.

Resonance: Natural oscillation frequency of a circuit, etc.

Scanning: Regular motion to take in an arranged area.

Sonar: Sound Navigation And Ranging.

Stage: One unit or section of amplifier, etc.

Telemetry: Relaying instrument information to a distance.

Ultrasonics: Operating methods beyond the range of hearing.

Watt: Unit of power.

INDEX

TITLES IN THIS SERIES

Arts
Art Nouveau for Collectors/Collecting and Looking After
Antiques/Collecting Inexpensive Antiques/Silver for Collectors/
Toys and Dolls for Collectors

Domestic Animals and Pets
Cats/Dog Care/Dogs/Horses and Ponies/Tropical Freshwater
Aquaria/Tropical Marine Aquaria

Gardening
Flower Arranging/Garden Flowers/Garden Shrubs/House Plants

General Information
Aircraft/Beachcombing and Beachcraft/Espionage/Freshwater
Fishing/Modern Combat Aircraft/Modern First Aid/Photography/
Sailing/Sea Fishing/Trains/Wargames

History and Mythology
Witchcraft and Black Magic

Natural History
Bird Behaviour/Birds of Prey/Birdwatching/Butterflies/Fishes of the
World/Fossils and Fossil Collecting/A Guide to the Seashore/
Prehistoric Animals/Seabirds/Seashells/Trees of the World

Popular Science
Astrology/Astronomy/Biology/Computers at Work/Ecology/
Economics/Electricity/Electronics/Exploring the Planets/Geology/
The Human Body/Microscopes and Microscopic Life/Psychology/
Rocks, Minerals and Crystals/The Weather Guide